AN EASY STROLL

THROUGH

A SHORT GOSPEL

MEDITATIONS ON MARK

AN EASY STROLL

THROUGH

A SHORT GOSPEL

MEDITATIONS ON MARK

by Larry Parsley

A MOCKINGBIRD PUBLICATION
Charlottesville, VA

To Jaletta, with deep gratitude

CONTENTS

Introduction

The people were amazed at his teaching, because he taught them as one who had authority, not as the teachers of the law. (Mark 1:22, NIV)[1]

A mere twenty-two verses into his gospel, Mark records a key distinction that people have been making ever since: *Nobody talks like Jesus talks.* And for that matter, nobody acts like Jesus acts. In Mark's day, and in our own, there are plenty of teachers who lay down the law. Jesus is different and authoritative and powerful. This little book invites you to linger over those mysterious words and deeds of Jesus.

I write this to you, by the way, no matter how you might self-identify when it comes to Jesus. Maybe you, like me, grew up with as earnest an evangelical Christian upbringing as possible. Your higher-ups urged upon you something called a "daily quiet time." They measured your spirituality in how long these times of Bible reading and prayer lasted and in how many days you went without a miss. And still, despite all the legalistic competition you endured, you would ideally rather have some portion of your day devoted to God.

I write this to you, perhaps, a Christian of a decidedly non-evangelical sort. The whole idea of a daily devotional feels a bit quaint. But you know this. *Jesus is your guy*. Whatever else you think about the edifice of Christian piety, you would follow Jesus virtually anywhere. And perhaps that is why you have picked up this volume.

I write to you, especially, if you would firmly place yourself outside the Christian fold. This is the case with almost everyone Jesus encounters in this gospel. In some ways, I envy you, because you have a chance to meet Jesus fresh, to read this story bit by bit and to think brand-new thoughts about Jesus (and then to hear what a bought-in Christian type like me says about them).

If I had a magic wand (which I don't, but boy, it would come in handy sometimes), I would have you read this gospel as if you were the thirteenth disciple, hanging just outside the circle of the Twelve who most closely followed Jesus. Because that's who I think Mark intended as his primary audience, those people who were intrigued enough by the person and message of Jesus to turn aside from daily priorities and to turn toward him in attentiveness.

If you follow him, as his thirteenth disciple, there are some hazards. He will ask you questions you don't know the answer to, and you will feel stupid. He will call you out when you are dull and dim-witted and fail to grasp his parables and teachings. He will take it personally when you refuse to trust him. But nothing will stop his march to the cross on your behalf. He has something he desperately wants you to know, to have, to imbibe—something we Christians refer to as grace.

Paul Scott Wilson is a preeminent preacher of grace. On a recent podcast, he relayed a story about why preaching grace, and teaching preachers to preach grace, is so important to him.[2] His grandmother, he said, was the wife of a Methodist pastor, and they lived in a Methodist "manse" in Quebec. His grandfather was in his study on the second floor one day when she called from downstairs to tell him lunch was ready. After two tries and no answer, she walked upstairs to get him. The door to the study was closed, and as she placed her hand on the doorknob, she heard a clear voice say to her, "My grace is sufficient for thee" (2 Corinthians 12:9, KJV). When she opened the door, she discovered to her horror that her husband had died, slumped over his desk. But the words she had heard prior to opening the door she took to be a direct assurance of grace from God, words which not only sustained her through the extensive grief to follow but stayed with her during her entire life.

Most of us don't receive a word of grace in such an extraordinary way. Still, that story reminded me how grace feeds a deep and daily need. And even ordinary means, a little reading in the morning or at lunch or before bed, can deliver an extraordinary perspective and even strength to make it through the day.

And finally, a little note on how to read this book. The simple answer is that you can read this book however you would like. The readings are not dated or coded by days of the week. This book was made for you, not you for this book (cf. Mark 2:27!). So if you want to read one entry a day for the next however many days, that's great. If you want to read once a week on Sundays, go for it. If you miss a day (*when* you miss a day), so what? If a reading does not connect, and you want to hit a mulligan and read the next one, go for it! If it sits half-read on a nightstand gathering dust for months, and then is picked up again, well, God be praised! If you want to read it like a novel, I think that is well within your right.

My only wish, indeed a prayer, is that when you read it, you will discover someone who, as the people in Mark's gospel once remarked, "has done everything well" (Mark 8:37). May his love find you, speak to you, stabilize you, and sustain you as you trail those who trailed Jesus through the gospel of Mark.

Beginnings

(MARK 1:1-13)

The Irish novelist Roddy Doyle eulogized his fiction-writing countryman William Trevor this way: "Every word mattered, every sentence was its own big house."[3] If economy is a virtue, Mark is a virtuoso. He will take a mere thirteen verses to introduce the story and tell you why it matters. Thirteen verses in, we will be more than ready to hear what Mark's main character has to say to us. Only thirteen verses, yet each one a mansion.

JUST ONE STORY
(1:1-3)

The beginning of the good news about Jesus the
Messiah, the Son of God… (Mark 1:1)

Sometimes, when a movie begins, while the camera
pans across a crowded city street or an ambling river,
say, a narrator will offer a brief intrusion into the story
that is about to unfold. Every word is measured, clipped
even. The narrator relays only the most essential details
the viewer needs to know and then scrambles out of the
way so we can meet and fall in love with the characters
and follow breathlessly along with the unfolding plot.
Mark plays that role in the opening three verses.

But Mark does more than voice over the opening
credits. In one verse, Mark invents a new genre—something called a "gospel." This good news story has Jesus
as its protagonist. Mark knows his singular story is the
sum of many: Israel's story, the prophets' stories, and
ultimately God's story. Since venerable witnesses like
Isaiah and Malachi are hundreds of years old, and since
Mark says that this is only the "beginning," it gives every
indication of being a past/present/future story.

As you turn your ear toward this story, as first Mark
and then Jesus begin to pull you in, remember this. It
is many stories, and it is one story. Or better, it is many
stories coming together into one story. And your many

stories—the stories of your parentage and your birth and your childhood and your adolescence and your adulthood and your résumé and your public failures and your silent regrets and your secret hopes—can also be folded into this one story, with Jesus as the protagonist. Remember, this is only "the beginning of the good news."

> *Jesus, enfold the meandering plot of my life into the good news story you are writing.*

THE OPENING ACT
(1:4-8)

*And this was his message: "After me comes the
one more powerful than I, the straps of whose
sandals I am not worthy to stoop down and
untie. I baptize you with water, but he will
baptize you with the Holy Spirit." (1:7-8)*

I would have easily followed him, if he would have
allowed it. John the Baptist, I mean. He is just so exotic,
isn't he? Forget the Temple—he sets up camp in the
wilderness, like so many spiritual luminaries before and
since. And when someone preaches that boldly, cutting
through my moral rot and flimsy pieties like a butcher
with a cleaver? Yet still somehow holding out hope for
true forgiveness? Absolutely I would have followed the
herd, wading up to my waist out in the Jordan River,
babbling out my deepest regrets and pleading for those
hands to push me down under and pull me back up
again.

I would have easily followed him, just by looking at
him. Who dresses like that? At first glance it seems he
raided the costumes department at the museum of Biblical history. He looks like Elijah and talks like Jonah.
His words are this message in a bottle tossed by Israel's
past onto the shores of Israel's present.

I would have followed him. I'm a sucker for a guru. I would have followed him, but John prevents it. "After me…" Don't focus on me, John says, but on the one who comes after me. His worth overwhelms me. I bring you orange peels but he brings you the orange. I bring you water but he brings you the Holy Spirit. *Not me,* John says, nor any other preacher or writer or speaker or leader. I'm just the highway exit sign. "After me," that's when the real adventure begins.

> *"From the best bliss that earth imparts, we turn unfilled to Thee again." (Bernard of Clairvaux⁴)*

THE OTHER SIDE
OF THE CURTAIN
(1:9-11)

At that time, Jesus came from Nazareth in Galilee and was baptized by John in the Jordan. Just as Jesus was coming up out of the water, he saw heaven being torn open and the Spirit descending on him like a dove. And a voice came from heaven: "You are my Son, whom I love; with you I am well pleased."
(1:9-11)

In three verses Mark shows us both sides of the curtain. In the first verse, we see what anyone else sitting along Jordan's banks would have seen, whether they paid attention to it or not. A young man from Nazareth lines up with other penitents to participate in baptism. But in the second two verses, Mark takes us behind the curtain. He tells us what Jesus saw and heard. What he *saw* was the heavens being ripped open like an old thin sheet, and through the flapping and ragged edges emerges the Spirit, circling like a dove in a stadium before coming to rest upon Jesus. And what Jesus *heard* was the Father, gushing. "You? You are my Son! Yes! And I love you! And I absolutely could not be more pleased with you than I am at this very moment."

It's almost too much, this atmospheric ripping and dove-like descent, the overly affectionate words. We don't know whether to turn our heads away in fear or embarrassment, or crane our necks to catch every scene and syllable.

As we go on this journey with Jesus, he will daily proclaim that there is, in a fact, a curtain. We "see through a glass darkly," yes (1 Corinthians 13:12, KJV). But there is something on the other side of the glass. And while we trudge along each day, even our most holy moments—the tap water of baptism and the gluten or gluten-free bread of communion—as mundane as they can seem, point to a deeper reality behind the curtain. Behind the curtain, the Father, Son, and Spirit play together in brilliant choreography and unashamed affection. Behind the curtain, we hear what Grace says to us. Because Grace believes that what God speaks to Jesus, he speaks through Jesus to us. "You are my child. I love you! In you I am well pleased!"

Jesus, you are our gateway to the
Father's blessing.

JESUS IS DRIVEN
(1:12-13)

At once the Spirit sent him out into the wilderness, and he was in the wilderness forty days, being tempted by Satan. He was with the wild animals, and angels attended him. (1:12-13)

If we were tempted to typecast the Spirit from the previous reading as a *mere* dove, a gentle sidekick always up for Jesus' adventures, our first verse of this brief reading startles us. The Spirit "drives" Jesus out into the wilderness, for nothing less than a forty-day-long assault by Satan.

Mark leaves it to the other gospel writers to tell you about the subtleties of these assaults, how each temptation aimed toward a perceived vulnerability of Jesus. It is enough for us to know that the setting (desert) was stark, the duration (imagine a wilderness fast that began on Thanksgiving and lasted through New Year's Day!) felt endless, and the company (Satan and the wild animals) was treacherous.

Often, the word "driven" can well describe you and me, dear readers. What drives us, though, is not the Spirit but comfort or ambition or vengeance or a whole host of other gremlins. There is a chance that any one of these dark forces has already been shaping our understanding of what today's agenda should be. This is the force of self-interest that drives us constantly. But Jesus signals for us early on in this book that his path will be anything but selfish. He will follow the lead not of his inner appetites but of the Spirit's bracing call, out into the wilderness, out among the wild, out into the arena, with only the angels to brighten his day. This is the trajectory that follows the lead of the Spirit to the cross. Grace could follow no other path.

Jesus, your grace redeems my drivenness.

The Gospel on the Road

(MARK 1:14-45)

One year Santa placed a yellow ten-speed bicycle under my family's Christmas tree and affixed my name to it. For a moment, I sat stunned. Then I sat on the bike, feeling the serrated imprint of the pedals on my bare feet. It was all I could do to wait for everyone else to open all of their presents. When a considerate amount of time had passed, I posed the question: "Can I take it outside?" Picture a boy, in pajamas and house shoes, out on a residential street in early morning, the chilly air rushing past him as he switched from first to second to third gear.

As we begin a new section of Mark's gospel, I find myself in a similar position. As impressed as I am by witnesses like Malachi and Isaiah and wooly John the Baptist, as moved as I am by Jesus' baptism and temptation, I can't wait to see what happens when Jesus takes this gospel out on the road. I want to see what it does on the seashore and in the synagogue, on crowded streets and lonely retreats, with beloved family and wretched outcasts. *Jesus, can we take the gospel outside?*

"THE TIME HAS COME"
(1:14-15)

After John was put in prison, Jesus went into Galilee, proclaiming the good news of God. "The time has come," he said. "The kingdom of God has come near. Repent and believe the good news!" (1:14–15)

A preaching professor of mine once offered a maddening bit of counsel. "Your first sentence has to grab them, or else they will be lost for the rest of the sermon." I cringe to think of how many first sentences I've wasted with "open your Bibles to" or "our passage for today" or some other purely functional but hardly arresting opening gambit.

Jesus must have been some preacher, because he opens with these brief words: "The time has come." Putting aside for the moment the fact that in other contexts these words could be anything but inviting (say, when spoken by a surgeon or judge or especially an executioner), in this context, these words defeat all the other "time" sentences we have lived with all our lives.

In many areas of our lives, we may think, "The time has passed." Once, there was a window of time in our lives where possibilities were laid out before us like steaming dishes at an all-you-can-eat buffet. *No longer*, we tell ourselves. This is the siren of regret who daily sings her mournful song over us. Another siren, cynicism, nightly serenades us as well. She sings, "The time will never come." In other words, that Great Pumpkin you spent so much of your childhood pining for is a myth.

But Jesus says, "The time has come." A new kingdom is passing so close by you can feel its brush at your elbow and breeze on the back of your neck. The kingdom belongs to Jesus, is Jesus, and now is ours. "The time has come…" at last.

Thank you, Jesus, for redeeming what feels like the lost days of our lives.

GOSPEL BAND OF BROTHERS
(1:16-20)

"Come, follow me," Jesus said, "and I will send
you out to fish for people." (1:17)

So here's the way it worked, on my playground at least. Two older and very athletic boys would select themselves as team captains. And then they would have a draft for the best available basketball players around. The tallest and quickest and most agile would go first, in rapid succession. And then, the agonizing choices. Who would they have to take now among these leftovers? The captains would practically hold their noses as players nine and ten were selected. And if you were number eleven? You can watch if you want, but you cannot play.

In this passage, there is only one captain. And his choice of four brothers is not based on their ability. As the rest of the book will show, Peter can be hotheaded and feckless, and those Zebedee brothers will have delusions of grandeur completely out of step with their humble Master and His mission. But the captain is not choosing them based on their qualifications, but rather upon *his* qualification. He knows where he is going, he knows what he wants to do, and he does not want to have all that fun of "fishing for people" (really, *rescuing* people) all by himself. *Come, follow me.*

Two brothers leave businesses and equipment and,

in the case of James and John, a father and a boat with "Zebedee and Sons" painted across the bow. It is a first lesson that in Jesus' kingdom, the grace we gain will always dwarf the good things we lose in the process. It is the first time that brothers from different mothers will discover what it means to truly become a *gospel band of brothers*.

And what about you, Number Eleven (if I may so indelicately put it)? He is walking straight in your direction today. As far as you know, you're his first-round draft pick. "I choose you."

> *Jesus, your choice of me overshadows life's rejections.*

GOSPEL WORDS
(1:21-27)

"Be quiet!" said Jesus sternly. "Come out of him!" The impure spirit shook the man violently and came out of him with a shriek. The people were all so amazed that they asked each other, "What is this? A new teaching—and with authority! He even gives orders to impure spirits and they obey him." (1:25–27)

One Sabbath day in Capernaum, folks who had just walked to the synagogue prepared to listen to some rabbi tell them something they likely already knew about some portion of some Old Testament scroll. But not this Sabbath. No one would forget this Sabbath. These words amaze the crowd and provoke at least one unfortunate, demonized listener. Throughout the gospels, the demons possess the best military intelligence on the threat Jesus represents to their mission. They "fear the Lord," ironically enough. They address him with strikingly accurate names like "the Holy One of God," even as they oppose him and terrorize those he came to rescue. They have no missile defense system that can handle the preemptive strike of his teaching.

Christ's words are no ordinary words. These are fresh words undergirded by unusual authority: "Be quiet! Come out of him!" (v. 25). These words do things—they expel and propel. These words will "uproot and tear down," "destroy and overthrow," and "build" and "plant" (Jeremiah 1:10).

I once heard a woman say, "I've probably gone back and listened to that sermon at least sixteen times." That sermon (not mine) must have somehow smuggled the fresh and authoritative words of Jesus into her soul. And she knew she dare not forget those words. Such words are eternally new and strong. They contradicted so much of what her worried soul had previously droned on and on about in her internal dialogue. And she knew that she had heard something eternally strong and new. "What is this? A new teaching—and with authority!"

Jesus, your words speak fresh power
into our lives.

GOSPEL TENDERNESS
(1:28-34)

That evening after sunset the people brought to Jesus all the sick and demon-possessed. The whole town gathered at the door, and Jesus healed many who had various diseases. He also drove out many demons, but he would not let the demons speak because they knew who he was. (1:32–34)

Several things flee in this passage. That fever that confined Peter's mother-in-law to her bed? With Jesus' touch it flees, and she rises to serve. When the "whole town" gathers at Peter's back door with their sick in tow, how many illnesses flee as well at the touch and command of Jesus? Jesus cannot turn these poor people away. Many demons scamper as well, struck dumb as Jesus drives them out of their victims. He will not listen to their sinister hymns (even if they do correctly point to his otherworldly power).

But something else has run away now, and that is Jesus' privacy. From now on, Jesus will have to fight for solitary moments with God and with his closest companions. The crowds will haunt him—at times showering him with praise, and toward the end of this book, sliming him with vitriol. And in his final moments on this earth, he will live out his dying agony in front of the throng.

Your temperament may differ sharply from mine, but I read Mark's words through the lens of an introvert, someone who craves time alone like oxygen. And I simply cannot imagine what it feels like to be Rock Star Jesus. And even if you are the extrovert's extrovert, even if you talk to the cereal boxes on lonely grocery aisles, even you must feel the cost that Jesus pays to be Jesus. From now on, Jesus will be hunted by friend and foe alike. And we must see, we must somehow feel down deep, that he willingly makes himself prey for you, for me.

Jesus, your sheer availability is but one deep
evidence of your love for us.

GOSPEL PRIORITIES
(1:35-39)

Simon and his companions went to look for him, and when they found him, they exclaimed: "Everyone is looking for you!" Jesus replied, "Let us go somewhere else—to the nearby villages—so I can preach there also. That is why I have come." (1:36–38)

In his introduction to *The Jesus Way: A Conversation on the Ways that Jesus is the Way*, Eugene Peterson notes how the popular acronym WWJD (What would Jesus do?) is "not quite accurate."[5] The key question is, *"How does Jesus do it?"* If the ends do not necessarily justify the means, what are the means Jesus employs? Peterson makes the point that if the American church thinks it can present the Jesus *truth* in the *American way* and somehow bring people the Jesus *life* (John 14:6), we are far from the mindset of Jesus.

Case in point: Jesus has been dominating the local headlines in Capernaum. Synagogue exorcisms, amazing preaching, long lines of sick being healed. A modern-day pastor like me, in the face of such contemporary metrics of ministerial success, would be tempted to camp out in Capernaum for a long time.

Jesus pursues a different way. Rising early after a late evening, foraging for solitude before the town awakens, Jesus has some kind of mysterious and clarifying conversation with his Father. When his exasperated disciples finally find him, they give him that indictment that is a contemporary verdict of both importance and misery: "Everyone is looking for you!" (v. 37). *You are a big deal, Jesus. You have an audience now, and your audience needs you.*

Jesus pursues a different means to become "successful." Jesus has more places to go, more people to introduce to his message of the kingdom. "That is why I have come" (v. 38). What a gift—to know why you are here on this earth. And for Jesus, what a fearsome responsibility.

Jesus, you teach us that our success is not based on what we do.

GOSPEL WILLINGNESS
(1:40-45)

A man with leprosy came to him and begged him on his knees, "If you are willing, you can make me clean." Jesus was indignant. He reached out his hand and touched the man. "I am willing," he said. "Be clean!" Immediately the leprosy left him and he was cleansed. (1:40–42)

I have seen it happen a hundred times. During office small talk in the mornings, you ask a coworker how they are doing, and they tell you they woke up sick. Why they still came to work is one of life's mysteries. Still, while trying to show conversational compassion, your mind is seized with a desire to see how quickly you can evacuate from this zone of contagion and bathe your hands in sanitizer.

Take that feeling and amplify it exponentially. A man on his knees, with leprosy (!), begging, mere feet away from you. And although we're only a few dozen verses into the gospel of Mark, we have come to believe that what this leper says to Jesus is empirically true: "If you are willing, you can make me clean" (v. 40).

Two things follow in rapid succession. First, Jesus penetrates the sick zone, touching the untouchable, combining sincere willingness with healing power.

Second, the now-healed leper defies Jesus' demand to keep quiet about the miracle; instead he "talked freely, spreading the news. As a result, Jesus could no longer enter a town openly but stayed outside in lonely places" (v. 45). Jesus will now be doomed to live on the edges of society, and even those efforts won't be successful ("Yet the people still came to him from everywhere").

Here is the cycle we see lived over and over again in our interactions with Jesus. Jesus pays the price for the cleansing he delivers to us.

Jesus, we celebrate your willingness to make us clean.

Mercy Does Battle

(MARK 2:1-3:6)

What follows in the next five readings is a battle between the Mercy that Jesus brings and the Religion that opposes him. The part of Mercy is played exclusively by Jesus, who extends compassion to the sick and scorned and spiritually lax. And Religion is variously played by a mixed bag of religious leaders—teachers of God's Law, a popular lay movement of rigorous Bible people called Pharisees, and even some disciples of Jesus' cousin John the Baptist. It is not surprising to me that Religion has formed such a broad coalition. And I am not unsympathetic to those scholars who claim that Pharisees and their like have been painted with too broad a brush by people like me. Surely, we can admire their devotion to learning the truths of the tradition and their zeal in following their understanding of what the Law requires.

Still, in each of the next five encounters, Jesus will bring a stinging rebuke to the forces of Religion, even as he defends those victims of its attacks.

And if you have been burned in the past by those who emphasize the blunt edge of the Law, or if you, like me, have colluded with such forces, the response of Mercy deserves our full attention.

MERCY SPEAKS
THE FIRST WORD
(2:1-12)

*Since they could not get him to Jesus because of
the crowd, they made an opening in the roof
above Jesus by digging through it and then
lowered the mat the man was lying on. When
Jesus saw their faith, he said to the paralyzed
man, "Son, your sins are forgiven." (2:4–5)*

The good news about Jesus spreads wildly through the
fishing village of Capernaum. Jesus is attempting to
lead a home Bible study, but the place is so packed it
feels like a department store on Black Friday. Still, Jesus
preaches until sunlight and dry reeds begin to fall upon
his head. Four men have literally "unroofed the roof"
and are lowering a friend down to Jesus.

What I hope and expect Jesus to say when he sees
the victim is, "Arise, take up your mat, and walk!" But
that is not what he says (at least not at first). What he
says is, "Son, your sins are forgiven." You can almost feel
the air rushing out of the balloon, can't you? That's it? A
paralyzed man lies on a mat before a miracle worker and
the first thing he hears is that his sins are forgiven? Yet
the more I reflect on this story, the order of Jesus' words
is absolutely right. Mercy speaks the first word. Before
Jesus fixes us, he forgives us.

In her book on writing, *The Getaway Car*, Ann Patchett discusses the crucial role forgiveness plays in the act of writing. She speaks of the inevitable letdown of not being able to execute the pristine vision of the book that resides in the writer's head. "I believe that, more than anything else, this grief of constantly having to face down our own inadequacies is what keeps people from being writers. Forgiveness, therefore, is key."[6]

This wisdom far exceeds the writing life. In every aspect of life, what we need, and need constantly, is for forgiveness to speak the first word: "Daughter/Son, your sins are forgiven." Actually, Mercy speaks not only the first word but the middle and the final word. *Lord have mercy, Christ have mercy, Lord have mercy, Amen.*

Jesus, may your mercy be the first word our souls hear today.

MERCY FIGHTS FOR LOSERS
(2:13-17)

When the teachers of the law who were Phar-
isees saw him eating with the sinners and tax
collectors, they asked his disciples: "Why does
he eat with tax collectors and sinners?" On
hearing this, Jesus said to them, "It is not the
healthy who need a doctor, but the sick. I have
not come to call the righteous, but sinners."
(2:16–17)

If you are trying to discern a pattern in the kinds of
disciples Jesus enlists for his mission, good luck. Earlier,
it was seasoned, ruddy-faced fishermen, and he hooked
them with an opportunity to do a new kind of fishing.
Now, teaching and traveling along the shore of the Sea
of Galilee, he makes eye contact with Levi, a hated tax
collector, an outsider to polite religious circles. Two
words—"follow me"—convince Levi to leave his ledger
books and follow Jesus. Before he leaves town, Levi per-
suades Jesus to follow him to his home for a party with
his disreputable friends. Apparently, Jesus is a magnet
to these folk. Those who assume their life choices have
exiled them from the life of faith are now sitting elbow
to elbow with Jesus.

Jesus' opponents cannot help but notice, and they
learn an early lesson when gossiping about Jesus—his

hearing is extraordinarily fine-tuned (v. 17). Why does he eat with "sinners"? Apparently, Jesus sees himself less as the President of the Holiness Club and more as an emergency room physician, binding up the wounds of those whose moral injuries are long past hiding.

Years ago, at a heated church business meeting, an older man rose to take issue with our pastor and the many changes he had made to reach people who don't go to church. This man complained how new neighbors from highly churched backgrounds were not interested in our church anymore. And then he leveled what he must have thought was his most devastating indictment: "Since you came to be our pastor, the wrong kind of people are coming to our church."

Exactly.

Jesus, thank you for welcoming the wrong kind of people…like me.

MERCY FIGHTS RELIGION - A
(2:18-22)

> *Jesus answered, "How can the guests of the bridegroom fast while he is with them? They cannot, so long as they have him with them. But the time will come when the bridegroom will be taken from them, and on that day they will fast." (2:19–20)*

I'm certain I won't get the story exactly right, but I remember hearing a preacher in my youth create a parable. In a pre-Internet era, a couple dated long-distance, he in his first year of college and she in her last year of high school. The only way they could communicate was through the writing of letters, which they did religiously as a way of keeping their love alive. Each one savored the letters they received, these beautiful tokens of love. Then, it was Christmas break, and finally a chance for the lovers to be reunited. But instead, the boy decided to stay at college and spend time re-reading the letters!

The preacher, I'm sure, was trying to warn us Bible nerds away from "Bibliolatry" (basically, worshiping the Bible). This problem—elevating the secondary over the primary—is a peculiar vulnerability of religious practice. We find it present in every generation, including the one in our passage. The religiously earnest Pharisees, along with John the Baptist's followers, are practicing a solid religious discipline of fasting. Their self-denial is laudable in some respects, and we know that Jesus himself fasts. But fasting and other earnest religious rituals are never the ends in and of themselves. And Jesus will not be confined to the old and brittle wine skins of mere asceticism. Fasting is designed to stoke a hunger that only Jesus can fill, the Jesus who is currently feasting with his disciples. Why read old letters when you can celebrate with the Beloved?

Jesus, your presence is the feast our legalistic souls are starving for.

MERCY FIGHTS RELIGION - B
(2:23-28)

Then he said to them, "The Sabbath was made
for man, not man for the Sabbath. So the Son of
Man is Lord even of the Sabbath." (2:27-28)

In Mark's gospel, the religious leaders often resemble
that state trooper who has parked his vehicle just off the
highway behind a cusp of trees. By the time you see him
as you speed down the road, it is too late. You will be
pursued, and you will be ticketed. It is inevitable.

In this passage, the Pharisees busted Jesus' disciples
for a major Sabbath infraction. The disciples were popping heads of grain by hand because they were hungry.
But "popping" is a cousin to harvesting, and harvesting
is work, and work is outlawed on the Sabbath. "May I
see your license and registration please?"

Pharisees don't die; they just shape-shift into new
incarnations—earnest Sunday School teachers, angry
pastors, nosy neighbors. Most of us can identify an inner
Pharisee lurking within our hearts as well (and if we
cannot, we are probably not looking hard enough).

What Jesus does next is play a kind of defense
attorney for the disciples and for the notion of Christian freedom. He first deconstructs the Pharisees' argu-
ment—*if our great forefather David could feed his hungry*
men the consecrated bread reserved for the priests, I think

my hungry disciples can be excused for eating a few heads of grain on the Sabbath.

Then Jesus reconstructs the true meaning of Sabbath. The Sabbath day, a day of rest and reflection and enjoyment that mirrored God's pattern of creation, was never intended to be a hoop for people to jump through. It is not primarily a day of "no's" or extreme self-denial. Rather, the Sabbath is a gift, hand-crafted for worn-out humans, by the one who invented it—"the Lord" of the Sabbath (v. 28). In this way, Jesus helps us revision even the most forbidding parts of Christian practice into what they truly are…gifts.

> *Jesus, your Sabbath is a gift our sleepy souls*
> *are waiting for.*

MERCY FIGHTS RELIGION - C
(3:1-6)

He looked around at them in anger and, deep-
ly distressed at their stubborn hearts, said to
the man, "Stretch out your hand." He stretched
it out, and his hand was completely restored.
Then the Pharisees went out and began to plot
with the Herodians how they might kill Jesus.
(3:5–6)

I'm the conciliatory one. I'm not necessarily bragging or apologizing about it, but when tempers flare at a meeting or dinner table, I'm usually the one who jumps into the fray and tries to get everyone to *calm down*. In this passage, I'm pretty sure Jesus would not appreciate my diplomatic intervention.

What is more than clear is that Jesus will not back down from a worthy fight. As we see again and again, Mark does a beautiful job of bringing out the emotional life of Jesus. Jesus looks around "in anger" and is "deeply distressed" at the stubbornness of those who refuse to answer his devastating questions about sickness and healing and the true purpose of the Sabbath. Then Jesus acts suddenly. He tells the man to do the impossible—to stretch out an inflexible hand—and complete restoration accompanies the man's simple response.

And here, not even three full chapters into a

sixteen-chapter gospel, the plot to kill Jesus is launched. In the case of Mercy vs. Religion, Mercy wins this round. Religion, however, is not close to finished. As verse 6 tells us, "Then the Pharisees went out and began to plot with the Herodians how they might kill Jesus." Thus, this case will ultimately be resolved at Christ's cross.

Jesus, healing comes at the deepest price.

A New Kind of Family

(MARK 3:7-34)

My church used to take us on "choir tours" when I was in high school. We would pile in a bus, drive to a distant church where our music minister was friends with their music minister, perform a Christian concert for the few faithful church members who assembled, and then stay in various homes of church members. The assignment to these homes felt as random as a lottery. One of the hardest experiences was hearing the next morning from the guy who stayed at the house with the pool and pool table and four beautiful daughters, while you stayed with the senior adult couple who placed you on a hide-a-bed and turned out the lights at 9PM.

I can't help but feel that in Chapter 3, Jesus is redefining family. He invites just about everyone who will let him over to his house. And not just to stay the night. In this chapter, we will begin to see: we just won the lottery.

LOVING ON THE RUN
(3:7-12)

*Because of the crowd he told his disciples to
have a small boat ready for him, to keep the
people from crowding him. For he had healed
many, so that those with diseases were pushing
forward to touch him. (3:9-10)*

When I was a kid there was a cartoon based on the
Beatles, and just about every episode had a scene where
John, Paul, George, and Ringo were on the run, with
energized fans dashing wildly in their direction. If anything, this scene feels more desperate. Jesus has now
gained a regional following. His retreat to the lake suddenly becomes very crowded. Jesus asks his disciples to
secure a small boat for his physical protection ("to keep
the people from crowding him"). His healings caused
the people to keep surging forward, backing him into
the sea. You don't have to suffer from claustrophobia to
feel the terror of this scene. There is one Jesus, and thou-
sands of seekers, each wanting something from him.
Jesus healed on his heels.

Once at my church, when we were renovating our
offices, I tried to relocate to the most-out-of-the-way
Sunday School classroom to study and have some time
alone. A church member who was helping us clean our
facility spotted me one morning and shouted: "There

you are!" I can guarantee you that what I felt at that moment was not the sheer joy of being discovered. Sadly, the needle of my compassion tank often hovers between a quarter of a tank and empty.

So Jesus simply astounds me. How do you not eventually hate your fans? How do you not grow to despise those who steal your time, steal your solitude, steal your personal space, steal your power? How do you keep shouting down the shrieks of the demons? How do you keep healing? How do you keep freeing the very people who are smothering you?

Jesus, even when your back is to the sea, you continue to welcome us.

A FAMILY OF DISCIPLES
(3:13-19)

*Jesus went up on a mountainside and called
to him those he wanted, and they came to him.
He appointed twelve that they might be with
him and that he might send them out to preach.
(3:13-14)*

One of the most morally ambiguous projects of the world of work is assembling a résumé. In doing so, I search over this life of ups and downs and cherry pick those handful of shiny gems—memberships and accomplishments—and I present them to you as if this is me. *What you see on these two pages, that's me, and I have only just begun to hit the highlights of the goodness I can bring to your company.*

When Jesus decides to "hire" his team of close work associates, he precedes the decision by a night of prayer at a mountain retreat (Luke 6:12). While the transcript of that prayer is hidden from us, we certainly don't imagine that Jesus and his Father were pouring over résumés, trying to find the best people and make the best work decisions. After all, he did select "Judas Iscariot, who betrayed him" (3:19). What is clear to me is that Jesus does not ask for résumés but rather builds them. He calls us so that we "might *be with him*"—as beautiful a membership as we could hope for. And he offers us his gospel power to share with others. Put that on your résumé.

Jesus, you honor us with the privilege of unconditional acceptance.

DYSFUNCTIONAL FAMILY REUNIONS AND NEW FAMILY UNIONS
(3:20-35)

"Who are my mother and my brothers?" he asked. Then he looked at those seated in a circle around him and said, "Here are my mother and my brothers!" (3:33–34)

Mark likes "sandwiches." He launches into one narrative (A), interrupts it with a new narrative (B), and then finally returns to the original narrative (A). The effect can seem at times like your old uncle chasing rabbits ("Now where was I?"), but with Mark there is artistry to it. As our passage opens, Jesus' biological family is deeply concerned about him. Admittedly, his new stardom is creating such a lifestyle crisis for him that normal patterns of daily living (and even eating) are interrupted. They look at Jesus, and out of either concern or jealousy, conclude that his spirit is somehow *broken* and that he needs to be rescued from himself.

Immediately, the camera shifts to Jesus' "academic family" (if I might loosely refer to the fellow teachers who regularly spar with Jesus over doctrinal issues). These experts profess no motivations of warmth or concern. To them, Jesus' spirit is not broken—it is *evil*. They want him kicked out of the guild. His exorcisms are inside jobs, they say. Jesus himself teaches and models an ever-expanding circle of love, one which certainly includes our biological families (i.e. our *nearest* neighbors) and also our enemies. Love, however, is not to be equated with capitulating to the family's ideology. Jesus makes clear that his spirit is neither broken nor evil; it is *holy.* And the Holy Spirit's work of redemption through Jesus will not only tie up Satan but defeat him.

When Mark brings us back to Jesus' biological family, we see that Jesus will not be rescued by his family; he will rescue them. He will invite them into a much larger spiritual family, adopted by grace. And all, including his biological kin, are welcome to join up.

Jesus, you place "the lonely in families."
(Psalm 68:6)

The Way He Operates

(MARK 4:1-34)

Sometimes, while lingering in a bookstore, I gaze in the direction of the children's section. Some visiting author or store employee has gathered children and their parents together, holding out the illustrations of a book and using playful voices to render the dialogue. That scene is not too different from what Jesus does as Chapter 4 opens. He performs stories of farmers and seeds and birds and lamps and cup measures. His illustrations are simple and vivid, like good children's literature. But his message begs to be taken seriously by grownups and children alike. He is laying out the operating system of the Kingdom of God. *So gather around, children. Storytime is about to begin.*

HE PLANTS GOSPEL
(4:1-20)

"Others, like seed sown on good soil, hear the word, accept it, and produce a crop—some thirty, some sixty, some a hundred times what was sown." (4:20)

Jesus tells the lakeside crowd a farming parable to describe life in God's kingdom. The gist is: a lot of bad things can happen to a seed but one very good thing can happen. Later, Jesus privately tells his confused disciples that his parables have a way of quickening the spiritually hungry and confusing the spiritually satiated. Still later, Jesus provides the key to this specific parable: Satan, human fickleness, and the ways of the world all wage war on the gospel that Jesus seeks to plant in our hearts. But when the gospel takes root, oh boy, the fruit!

Admittedly, I often want Jesus to take that gospel of his and place his thumb and press it down into the two inches of topsoil that fill the Styrofoam cup of my heart. And a few days later, voila! *Look at me! A gospel orchard!* All that takes for granted the conspiracy of evil that absolutely hates the gospel and works furiously to steal it and scorch it and choke it. Yet what is still more remarkable is that, despite all the obstacles, Jesus still persistently scatters the gospel in all directions, including mine. And his gospel continues to take root! This is a promise to hear and take to heart. "Whoever has ears to hear, let them hear" (v. 9).

Jesus, you continue to plant the gospel into my cluttered heart.

HE BRINGS TRUTH TO LIGHT
(4:21-25)

He said to them, "Do you bring in a lamp to put it under a bowl or a bed? Instead, don't you put it on its stand? For whatever is hidden is meant to be disclosed, and whatever is concealed is meant to be brought out into the open." (4:21–22)

Revolutions happen when something suppressed and whispered becomes shouted and celebrated. In Martin Luther King, Jr.'s "I Have a Dream" speech, that hidden and suppressed idea was that all Americans, regardless of race, might rightly celebrate true equality and freedom: *"Let freedom ring from Stone Mountain of Georgia. Let freedom ring from Lookout Mountain of Tennessee. Let freedom ring from every hill and molehill of Mississippi. From every mountainside, let freedom ring."* So many of the brave souls who internalized King's message could not help but take to the streets with locked arms and faithful songs and stark signs proclaiming freedom for all.

The gospel is not hidden, like a lamp obscured by a bowl. As Jesus said in his first public proclamation, "The kingdom of God has come near" (1:15). The King's agenda is not some classified document reserved for a whispering few. This is public news, good news, and everyone's news. And those who try to give his good news away find even more of it poured into their laps.

Jesus, may your gospel be poured out among us today in full measure.

HE MAKES THINGS GROW
(4:26-29)

He also said, "This is what the kingdom of God is like. A man scatters seed on the ground. Night and day, whether he sleeps or gets up, the seed sprouts and grows, though he does not know how." (4:26–27)

My grandfather was a farmer and a rancher. His garden produced okra and potatoes and watermelons and the best tomatoes ever to adorn your dinner plate. When I would spend weeks with him in the summer, I was awed by all he knew about the weather and the soil, about mending fences and repairing tractors.

The successful farmer in Jesus' parable, however, is overwhelmed by what he does *not* know. Yes, you might be impressed as you drive past his farm and survey acre upon acre of fields white with grain. But the farmer knows himself to be a bit player in this grand operation. He scatters some seed, goes to bed, wakes up, has some coffee, and tries to make himself useful for another day on this earth. Lather, rinse, repeat. All the while, something is going on beneath the surface of the earth, but for the life of him, the farmer could not tell you what or how. "*All by itself* the soil produces grain…" (4:28). At the right time, the farmer will grab a sickle and then begin to bring in the harvest.

Jesus is giving us yet another angle to understand how his kingdom works. And if you are one of those "high control" kinds of people, you better brace yourself: the kingdom of God does not need you. The kingdom is not crossing its fingers, day after day, hoping that you make things happen. Christ's gospel will inevitably do its work, and even those most closely associated with the operation will have to admit they "do not know how" Jesus does it.

Jesus, your gospel works far beyond
our paygrade.

HE STARTS SMALL
(4:30-34)

*Again he said, "What shall we say the kingdom
of God is like, or what parable shall we use to
describe it? It is like a mustard seed, which
is the smallest of all seeds on earth. Yet when
planted, it grows and becomes the largest of
all garden plants, with such big branches that
the birds can perch in its shade." (4:30–32)*

It seems odd for Jesus to magnify the "small." In the
opening to John's gospel, Jesus teams up with his Father
to create the vast universe his people inhabit. In that
same gospel, you learn that Jesus came because he loves
the "whole world." In the book of Acts, Jesus discloses to
his disciples that their mission will extend to the "ends
of the earth." Jesus traffics in the Big. So why hold out a
palm and have his disciples strain to spot a tiny mustard
seed?

I feel like a slacker admitting this, but there is
something so comforting in this parable. I don't do "big"
nearly as well as I wish I did. Big resolutions in January
falter long before the beginning of February. The grand
love I wish to extend to the people in my life is eaten
away by selfishness and distractedness. An idealism that
once wanted to change the world now, more realistically,

wants to simply finish the race God has called me to run…or better, walk.

Elsewhere Jesus speaks of this "mustard seed" as an emblem of faith (Matthew 17:20). It is less a testament to the powers of our piety and more an indication of what Jesus can do with so little. Hands that will soon multiply loaves and fishes can do a similar transformation with our faith (which is in itself a gift). One day, as a testimony to Christ's power, and his alone, birds will nest in the tree that Christ grew out of faith's tiny seed.

*Jesus, we marvel at the way you dignify the
smallest of gestures.*

Such Power!

(MARK 4:35-5:43)

Have you ever had a conversation at a car rental place, when the hardworking employee is offering you so many insurance options to protect you from the risks of something happening to this car you do not own? As a risk-averse person, I am always tempted to purchase the full package—anything to mitigate against the unforeseen troubles which could overtake me in an unfamiliar city. In any case, the employee still forces me to initial all these places that announce to the world I am completely on my own.

As we continue to shadow Jesus through this gospel, he will take on much bigger risks than scratches and fender benders. His power confronts "acts of God" in nature. He faces down debilitating illness and demonic power and death itself. He does not prevent the risks we face, no matter what insurance we try to purchase for ourselves. Yet his power is seen most clearly in all those places we initialed, where we feel we are utterly on our own.

SLEEPING BEAUTY
(4:35-41)

*He got up, rebuked the wind and said to the
waves, "Quiet! Be still!" Then the wind died
down and it was completely calm. He said to
his disciples, "Why are you so afraid? Do you
still have no faith?" They were terrified and
asked each other, "Who is this? Even the wind
and the waves obey him!" (4:39–41)*

Once Elijah the prophet taunted the prophets of Baal
about their god's failure to respond to their prayers with
this zinger: "Maybe he is sleeping and must be awak-
ened" (1 Kings 18:27). You would be hard-pressed to
find a more devastating criticism of a divine being. Your
god is too frail to be relied upon.

So what do we make of the fact that in this passage,
when his disciples need him most, Jesus sleeps in the
stern in a storm? If you believe he is fully human (as well
as fully divine), you can well understand the factors that
would induce sleep after a long day of teaching publicly
and privately. Still, you would think the "divine thing"
would kick in at a time like this, when an angry storm is
swamping the little gospel ship of the disciples.

When they awaken Jesus, he angrily stills the storm
and then stuns the disciples: "Why are you so afraid?

Do you still have no faith?" (v. 40). The heart rate of the disciples climbs even higher in the aftermath of the miracle—"Who is this…?"

It seems to me that this bad news/good news dynamic is at play in much less dramatic ways in our daily lives. The bad news of life's storms is compounded by what appear to be snoring sounds coming from our supposed Savior. But the fact that he can sleep assures us that he is completely unafraid of what is currently terrifying us. And so, as Augustine says, we who have forgotten Christ's presence must "rouse him" and let him remind us that "even the winds and the sea obey him."

Jesus, you are completely unafraid of my storms.

THE OTHER SIDE OF CHAOS
(5:1-20)

*When they came to Jesus, they saw the man
who had been possessed by the legion of demons, sitting there, dressed and in his right
mind; and they were afraid. (5:15)*

If you first encountered this passage in a movie theater, you would not leave without getting your money's
worth. This passage combines so many elements that
make money at the box office. Take the man that Jesus
and company meet as they secure the boat on the "other"
side of the lake, the Gentile side. A man, whose fearsome appearance rivals any zombie or "white walker,"
steps out to confront Jesus. Chains dangle uselessly from
his wrists and ankles. He socializes with the dead, and
his fellow citizens have grown oddly accustomed to his
cries of anguish and his self-mutilation.

Or listen to the underworld conversations taking
place when the demons frantically bargain with Jesus.
Or watch the special effects of a herd of pigs, newly
filled with the legion of demons whom Jesus has cast
out of the man, now plunging into the sea. Or notice the
plot twist taking place among the townspeople: When
confronted with the good news about the man's healing
and the bad news about the pigs' drowning, the local citizens decide they can do without the disruption and beg

Jesus to take his traveling gospel show someplace else.

However, before you exit, I beg you not to miss two things. The first is the "after" picture of the one who, moments before, had lived a zombie's life. Now, this naked, roving, crazed man is seated, dressed, and "in his right mind" (v. 15). And don't forget the final commission either, where Jesus instructs the man to go back to his own people and share his gospel story, to "tell how much the Lord has done for you, and how he has had mercy on you" (v. 19). We don't have to experience the extremes this man did to crave the peaceful "right mind" that Christ creates and to embrace the freedom to gossip our gospel stories everywhere.

Jesus, may your gospel calm me, adorn me,
and place me in my "right mind."

POWER WON AND LOST
(5:21-34)

*At once Jesus realized that power had gone out
from him. He turned around in the crowd and
asked, "Who touched my clothes?" (5:30)*

Mark tells another of his sandwich stories, and today I
want to focus on the meat of the sandwich (leaving the
"bread" for later). In the middle of this section of Mark's
gospel, in the middle of a ridiculously eager crowd
pressing in upon Jesus, Mark puts his laser pointer on
one woman. If he had not, we would not notice her. Her
twelve-year illness has made her a social hermit. Her
life's work—financing a cure for her disease—has colos-
sally failed, leaving her more sick, more broke, more
miserable.

Yet once Mark points her out, our eyes are riveted.
We watch her skillful approach and her desperate out-
stretched arm that grasps the edge of Jesus' garment,
perhaps his prayer shawl. Two equal and opposite reac-
tions follow—she "felt in her body" that she was finally
free of her sickness, and he felt power exit him. It is,
from all appearances, a zero-sum game. Her gain is his
loss.

Years ago, when my wife was breastfeeding, we were
discussing the latest theories about breastfed kids having
a higher IQ or some such. "Yes," my fatigued wife said,

"and that's because the IQ points travel straight from the mother's brain into the infant's." Relatively early on in this gospel, we get a glimpse that the redemption Jesus offers us is no parlor trick, no mere snapping of fingers by some TV wizard. Redemption costs.

*Jesus, we are awed by the power that leaves
you to strengthen us.*

THE MINISTRY OF OVERHEARING (5:21-24; 35-43)

While Jesus was still speaking, some people came from the house of Jairus, the synagogue leader. "Your daughter is dead," they said. "Why bother the teacher anymore?" Overhearing what they said, Jesus told him, "Don't be afraid; just believe." (5:35–36)

Short story interpreters call it an "epiphany." It happens, often in the closing paragraph of the story, when the protagonist has some flash of insight about themselves or life. The synagogue leader Jairus has not one but two epiphanies in Mark 5. After going on his quest to find the only one who could save his dying daughter, after falling at Jesus' feet and begging him to come, after fighting through the oppressive crowd, Jairus hears the soul-crushing news from messengers sent from home. "Your daughter is dead. Why bother the teacher anymore?" Those words mixed bald truth (your daughter is dead) with deceptive implications (Jesus can't help, doesn't care, shouldn't be bothered). With harsh clarity, Jairus gets his first epiphany—the utter anguish and pointlessness of his errand.

But Jairus' story is not over. It takes its turn with Jesus "*overhearing* what they said" (5:36). Jesus responds by telling Jairus, "Don't be afraid; just believe," or literally, "No fear; only faith." In other words, Jesus "overhears" the soul-smashing and faith-defeating words spoken to Jairus and says, *Don't give your heart to their words. Listen to mine instead.* Later, taking Jairus' daughter's hand, Jesus says, "*Talitha koum!*" (Little girl, I say to you get up.) And she does. This second epiphany swallows the first, reversing the death sentence Jairus overheard from the messengers.

We deeply need Jesus to overhear those words that crush our unprotected souls—those dark epiphanies that we speak to ourselves (as much as hear from others). *You are a fraud. Your best days are behind you. If people really knew the real you...I doubt even Jesus can get you out of this situation.* Words like these punish our unguarded hearts.

> *Jesus, overhear our crushing epiphanies and*
> *create new ones through your gospel.*

Persevering Through Pain

(MARK 6-8)

When I was just starting my doctoral studies, an older pastor friend who had just finished his doctorate spoke words that stuck with me on my academic journey. "You don't have to be smart to get a Ph.D.," he said. "You just have to have a tough butt." His words were deflating, for I had hoped this external degree might provide some inner validation of an intelligence I knew I was lacking. His words may have lacked a certain pastoral elegance, yet their proverbial wisdom proved undeniable over time. This accomplishment, like most of life's accomplishments, would be sustained less by native ability and more by the grace of perseverance.

In these next three chapters (6:1-8:38), the Author of Grace will repeatedly demonstrate his persevering love for us. He will be rejected by his hometown, endure the assassination of his forerunner, face the continual faithlessness of his closest companions, and confront the continual battering criticisms of the religious professionals. By the time we reach the end of this section, Jesus will have set his sights squarely on the cross he will soon carry.

SHRINKING JESUS
DOWN TO SIZE
(6:1-6A)

"Isn't this the carpenter? Isn't this Mary's son and the brother of James, Joseph, Judas and Simon? Aren't his sisters here with us?" And they took offense at him. Jesus said to them, "A prophet is not without honor except in his own town, among his relatives and in his own home." (6:3-4)

When I came back from a summer camp having made public a desire to become a preacher, my home-church pastor wasted little time. A few weeks later, eighteen-year-old me was the guest preacher at my own church one Sunday night. As I remember it, my first sermon was on the subject of God, humanity, sin, heaven, and hell (and took all of about ten minutes). Still, those sweet people who had rocked me in the nursery and taught me in Sunday School as a child and taken me on Junior High retreats made it a point to come up to me afterwards and speak words of deep affirmation about God's hand on my future.

When Jesus preached an infinitely wiser sermon in his home synagogue at Nazareth, the reception was mixed. His reputation as a healer and his wise words were undeniable. Still, one of the sadder tendencies of our sinful selves is to use labels to shrink people down to our diminutive categories. *He's an egghead. She's one of those vegan-types. Let's just say his family is not the most "sophisticated."*

In Jesus' case, the shrinking sounds something like this: "Look, I don't care how jazzy his words seem to outsiders, we know this kid. We know his people—nice folks but not world-changers if you know what I mean. So let's tap the breaks a little on the Jesus Train..." So often, our labels betray our lack of faith that Jesus could truly surprise us.

> *Jesus, forgive us for trying to domesticate you.*
> *Be our "prophet with honor" today (v. 4).*

ALL I NEED
(6:6B-13)

Calling the Twelve to him, he began to send them out two by two and gave them authority over impure spirits. These were his instructions: "Take nothing for the journey except a staff—no bread, no bag, no money in your belts." (6:7–8)

Whenever a person in my social circle brings up Steve Martin's movie *The Jerk*, someone inevitably mentions the scene when the character played by Martin is breaking up with his girlfriend (Bernadette Peters). On his way out the door, a bathrobe-clad Martin declares that he doesn't need her and he doesn't need all their accumulated stuff. "I don't need anything. Except this." And he picks up an ashtray, and then a paddle game, and then a remote control, and matches, and a chair. Ultimately, his arms full of stuff, he trudges outside.

When Jesus begins to entrust his authority to the Twelve, he forces them to audit the things they really need. He strips them of items most of us would consider much more mission-critical than a paddle game or ashtray—things like food and cash and extra clothes. And yet, as they will discover, empty hands will soon anoint the sick and channel the healing power of the gospel.

Jesus' stark instructions—"Take nothing for the

journey"—hit me right where I live, for I am an over-packer. I pack every conceivable item of clothing and convenience because I can't bear the thought of being unprepared and far from home. Jesus persists in the stubborn belief that empty hands are more likely to be filled by gifts more valuable than anything else on our packing list.

Jesus, forgive my overly full hands, grasping at all the things I think I need, forgetful of the one thing I truly need.

THE GOSPEL WILL NOT BE
DECAPITATED
(6:14-29)

*King Herod heard about this, for Jesus' name
had become well known. Some were saying,
"John the Baptist has been raised from the
dead, and that is why miraculous powers are
at work in him..." (6:14)*

In a gospel noted for its brevity, we are given a lengthy
and gruesome digression that does not seem, at first,
to have anything to do with Jesus. In a gospel about a
heavenly kingdom, we depart for a moment to peer at
the ugly underbelly of life in an earthly kingdom. King
Herod (Antipas, the second son of Herod the Great)
had an uneasy relationship with John the Baptist, the
forerunner of Jesus. Herod found John's preaching both
puzzling and fascinating, except when the sermon was
on adultery. Herod's new wife Herodias, on the other
hand, was not so easily amused. Lashing out, she con-
spires to deliver John's head on a banquet platter.

So how does this darkly fascinating incident move
the Jesus story forward? Could it be that Mark wants
us to see Jesus getting a sneak preview of the fate that
awaits him by the rulers of this world? Perhaps. And
yet, rereading the opening words of our passage (vs.
14-17), we see that the story of John's assassination is

actually a flashback, and what brings the story so traumatically back to King Herod's mind is the news of the spreading of Jesus' kingdom (for "Jesus' name had become well known"). Herod even fears that John the Baptist has been raised from the dead. Apparently, you can decapitate the gospel preacher, but not the gospel. It still speaks.[7]

Jesus, your crucifixion is not the end of your story.

FEEDING THE FRUSTRATING
(6:30-44)

So they went away by themselves in a boat to a solitary place. But many who saw them leaving recognized them and ran on foot from all the towns and got there ahead of them. When Jesus landed and saw a large crowd, he had compassion on them, because they were like sheep without a shepherd. So he began teaching them many things. (6:32–34)

Once, on a bus on my last day of youth camp, an adult sponsor became overly frustrated with the constant shenanigans and disrespect on the back of the bus. Then she just lost it. "I hate you," she screamed. "I hate all of you!" At least she was honest.

One occupational hazard for anyone involved in any kind of ministry is that we begin to, at the very least, resent those we are called to serve. I definitely feel my inner irritation rise when I picture Jesus and those disciples slipping across the lake for a solitary getaway, only to be confronted by the same folks they fled from. Jesus' disciples come up with what feels like a tactful way of dealing with the situation. "Send the people away so that they can go…buy themselves something to eat" (v. 36). I love that answer: the disciples combine a professed concern for the people with a smooth pathway back to their intended retreat.

Jesus' response must have frustrated the disciples: "You give them something to eat" (v. 37). He forces them to take inventory and then blesses their pitiful rations as if they are some extravagant gift from God. And five thousand frustrating people are fed by Jesus, with twelve takeout boxes of leftovers (one for each resentful disciple?). Apparently, whether we deserve it or not, "He makes me lie down in green pastures... He restores my soul" (Psalm 23:2-3, ESV).

Lord Jesus, you grace us difficult sheep with a shepherd's care.

SEEING OUR STRAINING
(6:45-56)

*After leaving them, he went up on a moun-
tainside to pray. Later that night, the boat was
in the middle of the lake, and he was alone on
land. He saw the disciples straining at the oars,
because the wind was against them. (6:46–48)*

My dog Humphrey oscillates between bravado and anx-
iety. Should any dog from the neighborhood dare to
darken the sidewalk in front of our house, Humphrey
will race to the window beside our front door, barking
furiously at the intruder. Yet whenever Humphrey mis-
takenly thinks that all the humans have left the house,
he lets out the most heartrending yelp. I am no dog psy-
chologist, but he sounds completely bereft, as if he were
the last mammal on earth.

For us humans, suffering and fear have a way of iso-
lating us, of creating in us this terrible, anxious lone-
liness. That's the picture I have of these disciples, in a
storm on the Sea of Galilee. Jesus has sent them on
ahead in the boat while he prepares for a prayer retreat
on the mountain. It is now the Roman "fourth watch,"
the final watch of the night (somewhere between 3 and
6AM). It is hard to know which emotion the disciples
feel more keenly—fear that the storm they face might

engulf them, or fatigue from battling the storm most of the night.

The line that gives me deep hope is this: Jesus "saw the disciples straining at the oars" (v. 48). His vision of their plight prompts him to walk across the storm, scaring the disciples as he simultaneously pumps courage into them. The thought that Jesus sees from afar the strain in our biceps and hears the terror in our prayers speaks its own courage into our fears. Even when we are desperately alone, we are not alone.

> *Remind us, Jesus, that you see our "straining"*
> *today, especially when we are fearful and*
> *alone.*

LOOKING UNDER
PRISTINE RUGS
(7:1-23)

*He went on: "What comes out of a person is
what defiles them. For it is from within, out
of a person's heart, that evil thoughts come—
sexual immorality, theft, murder, adultery,
greed, malice, deceit, lewdness, envy, slander,
arrogance and folly. All these evils come from
inside and defile a person." (7:20–23)*

"Don't ever play poker with Jesus: he sees all the cards
you're holding." That's what I want to say to this dele-
gation of religious professionals from Jerusalem, those
hoping to make a citizen's arrest of Jesus' disciples
because they eat with unclean hands. The *law of holy
hand washing* is one of those add-ons, one of the addi-
tional laws to Scripture, which fall under the category of
"the tradition of the elders" (v. 3).

Jesus knows that these Pharisees, pristine on the
outside, have swept a considerable amount of moral filth
under the rug. They have figured out a way to win the
Ten Commandments game *and* cheat their parents in
the process (vs. 10-13). They have learned that reckless
game we might have learned in church, to make your
lips move in holy directions while your heart remains
free to pursue sinful fantasies (v. 6, citing Isaiah 29:13).

Like the Pharisees, we think we can have it all—social applause for our righteous reputations plus inner freedom to satiate our selfish longings.

This religious game would be so much easier if we could merely polish the surface of our lives. But Jesus declares that the true risk of contamination lies not from dirty hands but from filthy hearts. And what are we supposed to do about that, Jesus? It is not just the Pharisees who attempt to hide, among other things, "greed, malice, deceit, lewdness, envy, slander, arrogance and folly" (v. 22).

Jesus, cleanse it all, the inside and the outside of our lives.

AN UNCOMFORTABLE COMFORT
(7:24-30)

"First let the children eat all they want," he told her, "for it is not right to take the children's bread and toss it to the dogs." "Lord," she replied, "even the dogs under the table eat the children's crumbs." Then he told her, "For such a reply, you may go; the demon has left your daughter." (7:27–29)

If someone gave you the chance to "abridge" the gospels, what sections would you be tempted to remove? What offending stories would you rather not have to reconcile with your picture of Jesus? For me, at first glance, it would be this one. The text offends and sends me grasping for subtext.

TEXT: A desperate Gentile woman seeks the only one who can relieve her poor daughter of evil's grip. Jesus essentially says that he has a responsibility to feed his children first, and then take care of the pets later. Undeterred, the woman replies that "even the dogs under the table eat the children's crumbs" (v. 28). Jesus then pronounces freedom for the daughter, and when the woman returns home she finds her daughter healed.

SUBTEXT: Jesus' first mission had been to "feed" the Jews, and with that obligation fulfilled, he would direct his message around the world. Still, I believe that Jesus is being intentionally provocative with this Gentile woman. He is probing her heart, and he is thrilled with what he discovers. Her line about the "dogs under the table" shows that she gets it—she believes that with Jesus there is always more than enough grace to go around. Her words likely move Jesus to laughter, and demonstrably move him to action. "*For such a reply,* you may go…" Jesus manages, not just to heal the woman's daughter, but to celebrate her deep faith as well.

Jesus, move beneath the "text" of my day to
show me a deeper side of you and me.

UP CLOSE AND PERSONAL
(7:31-37)

After he took him aside, away from the crowd,
Jesus put his fingers into the man's ears. Then
he spit and touched the man's tongue. He looked
up to heaven and with a deep sigh said to him,
"Ephphatha!" (which means "Be opened!"). At
this, the man's ears were opened, his tongue
was loosened and he began to speak plainly.
(7:33-35)

Jerry Seinfeld famously called them "Close Talkers" (and if you are one, I mean no disrespect). Close Talkers draw frighteningly near to the people they are speaking with, penetrating a circumference that most people consider a proper social distance.[8] And by most people, I mean me. I'm perhaps overly conscious of breath—mine as well as the person speaking to me. When I am conversing with a Close Talker, I find myself trying imperceptibly to retreat, an inch here and an inch there—anything to regain some interpersonal safety.

In this passage, there is an intense amount of "close talking" going on. A man who can neither hear nor speak is brought to Jesus. And in one of the more unsanitary passages you will ever find in the gospels, Jesus takes the man aside and begins to stick fingers into the man's ears and rub his own spittle ("spittle" always sounds holier to me than "spit") onto the man's tongue. And then, looking up to heaven with a "deep sigh," Jesus cries out in his native Aramaic, "*Ephphatha!*"—"Be opened!" With that, the man's ears are opened and his tongue loosed. The townspeople cannot help but say of Jesus, "He has done all things well" (7:37, ESV).[9]

Some call this a "prophetic" miracle. In other words, the placement of this miracle near the center of Mark's gospel suggests that Jesus is doing *physically* for this man what he wishes to do *spiritually* for all people—to open their ears to the gospel. To do so, Jesus sidles up uncomfortably close to us, with *deep sighs* and profound prayers.

> *Jesus, speak closely to our souls as you cry,*
> *"Be opened!"*

JESUS DOESN'T SHOW HIS WORK
(8:1-10)

He told the crowd to sit down on the ground. When he had taken the seven loaves and given thanks, he broke them and gave them to his disciples to distribute to the people, and they did so. They had a few small fish as well; he gave thanks for them also and told the disciples to distribute them. The people ate and were satisfied. Afterward the disciples picked up seven basketfuls of broken pieces that were left over. (8:6-8)

My math teacher would get so upset with us, and we with him. We would hand him the quiz he had recently graded, show him that we in fact got the right answer to question #7, and query him as to why he gave us partial credit. His answer was always the same: "You didn't show your work."

In this passage, Jesus does not show his work. If the passage feels familiar, it should (see 6:30-44). This time, the large and hungry crowd is slightly smaller, but Jesus' compassionate reaction is the same. When he expresses his desire to feed this mass of hungry people he's been teaching now for three days straight, the disciples are stymied by the math problem (4,000 people + remote place + 7 breadsticks + a couple of sardines

= no catered lunch). Jesus, seemingly oblivious to their equation, seats the people and praises High Heaven for the meager rations the disciples have scrounged up. And then, somehow, in the distribution, Jesus solves the problem—four thousand people eat, and four thousand people are now "satisfied" (v. 8).

Jesus solves the problem, but he doesn't show his work. He shows us *himself*—a heart of compassion and an indomitable will to feed his sheep. And he shows us those hands, hands that break and bless and multiply. Hands that consistently reach out in our direction, to care for us and to bless us.

Jesus, take my meager life into your hands and multiply it.

WHAT HAVE YOU DONE
FOR US LATELY?
(8:11-21)

*The Pharisees came and began to question Je-
sus. To test him, they asked him for a sign from
heaven. He sighed deeply and said, "Why does
this generation ask for a sign? Truly I tell you,
no sign will be given to it." Then he left them,
got back into the boat and crossed to the other
side. The disciples had forgotten to bring bread,
except for one loaf they had with them in the
boat. "Be careful," Jesus warned them. "Watch
out for the yeast of the Pharisees and that of
Herod." (8:11–15)*

Of all the things Jesus could warn his disciples about,
why choose *yeast?* On the relatively few occasions I've
made bread, I marvel at what the tiny contents of that
yeast packet accomplish—turning the sodden mass of
flour and water and salt and assorted other ingredients
into this bubbling loaf.

Here, of course, Jesus speaks of the Pharisees. They
have witnessed or heard of one amazing miracle after
another—the sick healed, the demonized set free, the
bread multiplied. Still, they ask for yet another "sign

from heaven," hoping to expose Jesus for the fraud they pray he is. Jesus not only refuses their request but later warns the disciples against "the yeast of the Pharisees." The disciples (almost comically) think Jesus is talking about literal bread, left over from the previous miracle, which deeply frustrates Jesus.

So what is Jesus warning against? My best guess is this "yeast" points to the deadening nature of cynicism. A little lump of it can permeate our minds and hearts. It can render us dismissive or insensitive to the presence of Christ moving among us. It can cause us to miss out on or question the presence of grace that is distributed so freely to us. It diminishes the goodness of our past, and is always daring Jesus to do something definitive that will really cause us to jump on board with him. No wonder he "sighs deeply" (8:12).

Lord, have mercy on the inner cynic in
all of us.

TWO CHEERS FOR
PARTIAL VISION
(8:22-26)

*He took the blind man by the hand and led
him outside the village. When he had spit on
the man's eyes and put his hands on him, Jesus
asked, "Do you see anything?" He looked up and
said, "I see people; they look like trees walking
around." Once more Jesus put his hands on the
man's eyes. Then his eyes were opened, his sight
was restored, and he saw everything clearly.
(8:23–25)*

"I can see clearly now the rain is gone. I can see all
obstacles in my way. Gone are the dark clouds that had
me blind. It's gonna be a bright, bright sun-shiny day."
Johnny Nash wrote it (1972), Jimmy Cliff made it a hit
(1993), and seemingly everybody has covered it. The
song celebrates a clarity and optimism so often missing
from our day-to-day dreariness. For some reason, that
song from my childhood forms a kind of soundtrack as
I read this passage.

Many believe this story operates on two levels. In
Bethsaida, friends bring a physically blind man (likely
not blind from birth) to Jesus and plead for his healing.
As he does in a parallel miracle at the end of Chapter
7, Jesus takes the man away from the others and gets

uncomfortably close to the man (including spitting on his eyes!). Ultimately, the physical miracle is complete and the man "saw everything clearly" (v. 25). Yet unlike the other miracles of Jesus, this one doesn't happen instantly. At the first touch, there is partial vision (the people around the man are blurry figures in an animated forest). It took a second touch of Jesus for the man's eyes to be completely restored.

At a deeper level, Mark is giving us a picture of the disciples, and a picture of ourselves. In this world, our best hope is a partial vision of who Jesus is and what he is doing. Our vision is constantly clouded by our sin and frailty, by our doubt and distraction. But even blurry visions of Jesus are to be celebrated, a down payment for the day when we shall see him "face to face" (1 Corinthians 13:12).

Jesus, touch our eyes, again and again.

TURNING POINT
(8:27-33)

Jesus and his disciples went on to the villages around Caesarea Philippi. On the way he asked them, "Who do people say I am?" They replied, "Some say John the Baptist; others say Elijah; and still others, one of the prophets." "But what about you?" he asked. "Who do you say I am?" Peter answered, "You are the Messiah." (8:27-29)

There is that point, when swinging on a swing set, when time almost stops. You have swung back as far as the thrust of your legs will take you, suspended, before gravity careens you back toward the place from which you came. This is that moment in Mark's gospel. Jesus and his disciples have ventured far to the north from Jerusalem to a village called Caesarea Philippi. Soon, they will careen back toward Jerusalem, toward the cross.

In this moment in time, Jesus asks two questions. The first one is *academic* (who do others say that I am?) and the second is *personal* (what say *you?*). For a season in my twenties, I spent time in graduate school and local church ministry simultaneously. In graduate school, I could make high marks on my papers by simply surveying what a number of divergent voices had to say on a particular topic. But that approach did not work well in the local church. People didn't care so much what others had to say. They wanted to know where my heart was.

Peter takes a stab at the personal question, and at best gets partial credit. He rightly claims that Jesus is not merely one of the prophets from the past but is rather *the* Messiah whom God promised to rescue his people. Then, when Jesus agrees and begins to tell him of the necessary suffering the Messiah must endure, Peter the Pupil rebukes Jesus the Teacher. Peter wants a Messiah who will smite his enemies, while Jesus promises a Messiah who will die for his enemies. It was and still is the key question: "Who do you say I am?"

> *"I have a great need for Christ; I have a great Christ for my need." (Charles Spurgeon)*

A LOSER'S GUIDE TO LIFE
(8:34-38)

Then he called the crowd to him along with his disciples and said: "Whoever wants to be my disciple must deny themselves and take up their cross and follow me. For whoever wants to save their life will lose it, but whoever loses their life for me and for the gospel will save it."
(8:34-35)

Glory is a powerful motivator. Young athletes push themselves far beyond previous levels of endurance, all the while dreaming of a crowd standing on their feet, awash in thunderous applause. Some among us can push through pain and obscurity and countless roadblocks if we are assured that on the other side of the obstacle there is glory.

Jesus has a way of dumping a bucket of icy water on all our fantasies of success. For those disciples who dreamed of entering Jerusalem as cabinet members of their newly minted Messiah, Jesus proclaims a different and darker path. The milestones of their story will be measured out in losses and, well, crosses. Apparently, the Father glories in things the rest of us avoid at all cost (v. 38).

This way of Jesus takes quite a while to wrap your mind around—at least a lifetime or two. It is not the way we would write our personal entries in Wikipedia. "By the world's standards, Larry never really amounted to much, nor did the losers he hung out with." But it is the way Jesus chooses to write the gospel story: "For whoever wants to save their life will lose it, but whoever loses their life for me and for the gospel will save it" (v. 35).

Jesus, you lost it all for us.

Mountains and Valleys

(MARK 9:1-50)

If you're not careful, you can easily get whiplash following Jesus. As we'll see in this next section, at one moment, Jesus is standing on a mountain in blazing white holiness, a picture almost too glorious for earthly eyes. The next moment, he's stuck in the valley, complete with arguing disciples, a tortured child, and a half-believing father. In this section, Jesus will begin to prepare his disciples for his coming crucifixion (the deepest valley) and the ultimate mountaintop of resurrection.

The good news for us is that in our lives of breathtaking mountains and agonizing valleys (at times more like caves than valleys), Jesus is there. Wherever we are, Jesus is always there.

A GLIMPSE BEHIND
THE CURTAIN
(9:1-13)

*Then a cloud appeared and covered them, and
a voice came from the cloud: "This is my Son,
whom I love. Listen to him!" (9:7)*

Years ago a friend shared with me a story of his powerful
dream. In this dream he had a conversation with God,
and asked God all of his hardest questions about suffering in the world and suffering in his life. He distinctly
remembered God giving beautiful answers to all of his
questions. He used to keep a tablet by his bed, and he
said he didn't want to lose these insights. Waking long
enough to jot down the answers, he soon sank again into
a peaceful sleep. When he woke the next morning, his
first thought was to grab that tablet, only to discover
that all that was written on it was gibberish.

That story came to mind as I read again about Jesus'
transfiguration. Three of Jesus' close companions are
witnesses to the most dreamlike revelation of Christ's
true identity—his dazzling holiness, his easy conversation with Old Testament worthies (Moses represent-
ing the "law," and Elijah the "prophets"). They saw the
cloud, reminiscent of the visible glory that descended
with God's presence in the Tabernacle. And they heard
the ringing endorsement from God himself: "This is my

Son, whom I love. Listen to him!" (v. 7).

Of course, this epiphany would have to come to an end. This was not the time to transcribe the vision and share it with others (v. 9). Indeed, those three disciples were not quite sure what the vision actually meant anyway (v. 10). It was enough to know that the curtain had been pulled back, if only for a moment, and they had seen a breathtaking glimpse of the other side.

Jesus, give us the gift of faith to see a
deeper side of you.

AN HONEST PRAYER FOR FAITH
(9:14-29)

"If you can'?" said Jesus. "Everything is possible for one who believes." Immediately the boy's father exclaimed, "I do believe; help me overcome my unbelief!" (9:23–24)

I mentor a middle school boy over the lunch hour, and our rendezvous point is the cafeteria. While I wait for him, I marvel at the assistant principals and teachers who have lunch duty. There are so many students, and so few adults. They walk around with solemn faces, eyes peeled for the next round of hijinks or outbreak of violence.

I don't ordinarily picture Jesus as a middle school principal, but this passage bends my mind in that direction. As he descends from the mountain with Peter, James, and John, he finds chaos in the valley. The "teachers of the law" are arguing with the other nine disciples, who are in turn engaged in conflict with a distraught father over his demon-possessed son. These same disciples who earlier channeled the power of Jesus (6:12-13) have been utterly helpless with this afflicted boy. And Jesus must somehow attend to the chaos breaking out all around him—chaos connected one way or another to a lack of faith in Jesus.

Later, he will speak to his disciples about faith and

prayer. But the heart of the passage for me is found in this tender conversation Jesus has with the boy's father. Helplessly, the man asks Jesus to do something, *if* he can. Jesus takes exception to the "if" and urges the distraught dad to put his faith in him. "I do believe," the man says. "Help me overcome my unbelief!" What does this mean? It seems that belief and unbelief are often kissing cousins. Thankfully, our beautiful Savior believes for us, even as we struggle to believe in him.

Jesus, heal our unbelief, too.

BEAUTY AND BEASTLINESS
(9:30-37)

They came to Capernaum. When he was in the house, he asked them, "What were you arguing about on the road?" But they kept quiet because on the way they had argued about who was the greatest. Sitting down, Jesus called the Twelve and said, "Anyone who wants to be first must be the very last, and the servant of all." (9:33–35)

In these eight verses we find all the beauty and beastliness of the religious life. The ugly side is clearly on display. For the second of three conversations (see also 8:31-32; 10:33-34), Jesus is attempting to prepare his disciples for the hell that will be unleashed on him by the combined forces of church and state. The disciples respond to this shockingly bad news as I am sure I would have—with a mixture of misunderstanding, fear, and avoidance. Then Jesus displays the superhuman hearing of a parent discerning the children's mischief in a back bedroom. When he confronts the disciples about their infighting, they are forced to admit their own religious ambition to figure out which one of them was second in stature to Jesus.

When I was in high school, I spent a week at a Christian camp. This particular camp would award the two outstanding campers at the end of the week. How

I craved that award! How I wanted to be thought of as "Most Christian" or some award title only slightly less ridiculous.

Thankfully, the beauty of Christ shines brightly in this passage as well. We find it in the trajectory of Jesus' life as he redefines greatness as service. And we discover it in his object lesson with a child (v. 37). Is there a more beautiful picture of faith than that of a child welcomed into the arms of Jesus? A child welcomed, not because he was deemed "Most Christian," but simply because Jesus loved him?

Jesus, forgive our hurtful strivings and help us to rest in your arms.

THE MADDENING
OBLIGATION OF
COOPERATION
(9:38-41)

*"Teacher," said John, "we saw someone driving
out demons in your name and we told him to
stop, because he was not one of us." (9:38)*

There is a big part of me, when I read the first verse
in this passage (v. 38), which wants to laugh at how
preposterous it sounds. Here's my expansion on the
apostle John's statement to Jesus: "Master, we saw someone using your power to successfully free another person
of the hellish tyranny of Satan in their lives, and we told
that man by all means to cease and desist!" Yet a bigger
part of me wants to cry. Something deep in our religious
psyches wants to colonize Jesus, to reserve him exclusively for people like us. "We are the chosen, and our
creeds explain clearly why Jesus signed a non-compete
arrangement with us. We are the ones who best repre-
sent him in the world."

Sometimes, as a kid, I would be exposed to a rela-
tive whose views shocked my young sensibilities. When
I asked my parents about it, they would sometimes
make a statement that seemed to combine truth and

compassion. "You have to understand, son, that Aunt So-and-So's world is very small."

What this passage hammers home with me is how often *my* world is very small. And while no one has the liberty to stamp Jesus' name on their pet doctrines (Matthew 12:30), it is still true that Jesus' work will always be so much grander than me and my church and my denomination and my kind of Christian. Anything done in Jesus' name—from the dramatic act of healing to the mundane act of giving "a cup of water in my name" (v. 41)—does not go unnoticed by Jesus.

> *"He drew a circle that shut me out—Heretic, rebel, a thing to flout. But love and I had the wit to win: We drew a circle and took him in!" (Edwin Markham)*

WHEN JESUS SHOCKS US
(9:42-50)

*"And if your eye causes you to stumble, pluck it
out. It is better for you to enter the kingdom of
God with one eye than to have two eyes and be
thrown into hell..." (9:47)*

Flannery O'Connor was known for creating strange and
grotesque characters—a philosophical murderer called
the Misfit, for example, and a traveling Bible salesman
who steals a woman's wooden leg! In a book of her
collected essays, *Mystery and Manners*, O'Connor says
that when a writer and the reading audience share the
same beliefs, the writer "can relax and use more normal
means of talking to it." However, when there is a dis-
connect between writer and reader, "you have to make
your vision apparent by shock—to the hard of hearing
you shout, and for the almost-blind you draw large and
startling figures."[10]

I think it is safe to say that in this passage, Jesus
is shouting. He paints stark and scary figures with his
words—people drowned by millstones, followers maim-
ing themselves as they enter God's kingdom. Perhaps
Jesus is concerned that his hearers will think nothing of
misleading the children that he has been at such pains
to welcome into his kingdom (see verses 37, 42). Perhaps Jesus feels that some will find that the call to the

Kingdom of God requires too much sacrifice. Perhaps Jesus intuits that some will think his gospel is just one more menu item on life's buffet, and not a matter of life or death, heaven or hell.

Jesus, have mercy on us, spiritually blind and hard of hearing.

Jesus Doesn't Stay in His Lane

(MARK 10:1-52)

There's an old joke in the church circles I run in. When a preacher begins to leave the airy world of doctrine and sink down into the nitty-gritty of God's laws daily broken by us, people say that the "preacher has stopped preaching and gone to meddling."

Surely, Jesus is a meddler. As we'll see in Chapter 10, he won't leave us alone. He meddles with marriages, and with our treatment of children, and with our greed and ambition and naked need. Jesus does not stay in his lane. He constantly swerves in and out of our deepest attachments and struggles. At times, under the crushing weight of his impossibly high and holy standards, we'll want to cry out in exasperation with his disciples: "Who then can be saved?" (10:26). Thankfully, as we'll learn, grace is not something we manufacture. Instead, thank goodness, "all things are possible with God" (10:27).

NO SEPARATION
(10:1-12)

> *"It was because your hearts were hard that*
> *Moses wrote you this law," Jesus replied. "But*
> *at the beginning of creation God 'made them*
> *male and female.' 'For this reason a man will*
> *leave his father and mother and be united to*
> *his wife, and the two will become one flesh.' So*
> *they are no longer two, but one flesh." (10:5-8)*

In this much-debated passage on marriage and divorce, Jesus opens up several windows into the Bible's take on marriage:

God's idealism: In Genesis 2, God invents marriage as a means of creating a new entity, a new family, "no longer two but one flesh" (v. 8). His vision is beautiful, holy, and daunting.

Moses' realism: In Genesis 3, when sin enters the garden, marriage is adversely affected. Later, God's law given through Moses recognizes that human "hardness of heart" can and often does have a corrosive impact on marital unity (v. 5).

Religious cynicism: As I read this passage, Jesus was specifically addressing those who were cynically attempting to hide adulterous intent under the cloak of "lawful divorce" (vv. 11-12).

So where does this leave us? I find a passage like this is best read with tears of lament and prayers of hope. We lament the deep pain and disillusionment that so often accompanies marital breakdown. So many divorced persons I've spoken with through the years describe an agony consistent with the tearing of "one flesh." *I can't seem to stop crying. My future looks grim. How am I supposed to raise these kids on my own?*

Yet I also find room for great hope. A God who can create the beautiful gift of "two-in-one" marriage has also provided the grace to forgive and repair all those who have been wounded by marriage gone wrong. Through the cross, God has "joined together" Christ and his church, and no one can "separate us from the love of God that is in Christ Jesus our Lord" (Romans 8:39).

Lord Jesus, pour your mercy on the married and the unmarried.

THE LONG ARMS OF JESUS
(10:13-16)

When Jesus saw this, he was indignant. He said to them, "Let the little children come to me, and do not hinder them, for the kingdom of God belongs to such as these." (10:14)

I was on a mission trip in Peru, and the local pastor asked me at the end of a worship service if I would participate in the dedication of their newborn son. I walked on stage, held the child in my arms, closed my eyes, and prayed my best pastoral prayer. When I said "amen" and opened my eyes, the stage had become flooded with parents, holding young children of all ages, seeking a blessing. Why not? Who doesn't want a blessing for their child?

Yet Jesus' disciples see themselves as handlers. Jesus is very important (true), his time is very limited (true), and it is up to the disciples to help him sort through his priorities (false). The disciples rebuke the parents, and Jesus rebukes the "rebukers"! The disciples erect a barrier, but Jesus turns it into a bridge. In welcoming the children, Jesus makes the remarkable assertion that "the kingdom of God belongs to such as these" (v. 14). *To children? What have they accomplished for God? Some of these kids can barely say their own names, much less recite the Lord's Prayer.*

The promise is clear, and it is breathtaking! This kingdom Jesus leads "belongs" to those who have nothing to bring him except naked need and vulnerability. Children, certainly, but not *just* children. The arms of Jesus are long. And to those of us who totally lack anything of worth to bring to Jesus, he still opens his arms, places his hands upon us, and pronounces a prayer of blessing. After all, who doesn't want a blessing?

> *Jesus, place your blessed hands upon our*
> *waiting heads.*

"WHO THEN CAN BE SAVED?"
(10:17-31)

*The disciples were even more amazed, and
said to each other, "Who then can be saved?"
Jesus looked at them and said, "With man this
is impossible, but not with God; all things are
possible with God." (10:26-27)*

College sweethearts sit around a Christmas tree, passing out presents to each member of the family. The
boyfriend grabs a gigantic wrapped box and plops it
down in front of his girl. She wonders what in the world
can be in this box, but it turns out it's a smaller box,
and when she unwraps it, yet again a smaller box, until
finally she comes to a tiny wrapped rectangle—with an
engagement ring inside.

I think of that story when I read this passage, only
with a twist. A rich and earnest man approaches Jesus
with a question about eternal life. His soul is outfitted
in a series of beautiful moral wrappings—he loves his
wife and his parents, doesn't lie or steal or get anywhere
close to murdering somebody. If anybody deserves eternal life, we think, this outstanding specimen does. But
Jesus—who "looked at him and loved him" (v. 21)—sees
the hidden greed at the very center of that man's life, a
greed that holds his soul captive. When Jesus confronts
the man with the law of living generously, he withdraws

from Jesus with sadness.

The crushing power of the law prompts great fear in the hearts of the disciples: "Who then can be saved?" By implication, Jesus' words communicate, "No one… at least not by their own power." Saving ourselves is an impossibility, no matter how brightly robed we are in pious deeds. But thankfully, "all things are possible with God" (v. 27)!

Jesus, let your law kill us so that your grace may resurrect us.

READING STRAIGHT THROUGH
TO THE END
(10:32-34)

> *"We are going up to Jerusalem," he said, "and
> the Son of Man will be delivered over to the
> chief priests and the teachers of the law. They
> will condemn him to death and will hand him
> over to the Gentiles, who will mock him and
> spit on him, flog him and kill him. Three days
> later he will rise." (10:33-34)*

A friend of mine was a news anchor for a local televi-
sion station in Texas during the 1980s. She once told me
about delivering a news story on a gloomy environmen-
tal report that had recently been issued. She was reading through the sad litany about air quality and polluted
waters when suddenly the teleprompter just stopped.
Not knowing exactly what to say, she free-lanced the
following line: "Other than that, everything's okay!"

Despite the brevity of this passage, it is hard to
read it through until the end. For the third time in this
gospel, Jesus is predicting his imminent demise. With
Jesus "leading the way" (v. 32) toward Jerusalem and his
eventual cross, he lays out for the Twelve the grim reality that awaits. Jesus will be apprehended and delivered
to, of all people, Israel's "chief priests" and "teachers of
the law." They will do their religious part—condemning

Jesus to death. Then it will be the Romans' turn, since crucifixion was their specialty. The litany, as Jesus relays it, is as dreadful as it can be—mocking, spitting, flogging, killing.

Did the mental teleprompter for the disciples stop somewhere along the way? Could they even comprehend the agony awaiting Jesus, or understand that his coming pain was an act of atonement for their sins (and ours)? Still, Jesus wants them to read all the way to the end. "Three days later he will rise."

> *"Do not abandon yourselves to despair. We are the Easter people and hallelujah is our song."*
> *(Pope John Paul II)*

"GLORIOUS"
MISUNDERSTANDINGS
(10:35-45)

"What do you want me to do for you?" he asked. They replied, "Let one of us sit at your right and the other at your left in your glory." "You don't know what you are asking," Jesus said. "Can you drink the cup I drink or be baptized with the baptism I am baptized with?" (10:36–38)

They are grown men, James and John, but somehow I picture them as boys. Boys who are paying little-to-no attention to the prophecy of suffering Jesus has just unfolded (vv. 32-34). Boys who think they can get their spiritual father (Jesus) to agree to their request before hearing it (v. 35). Boys who dream of nothing but *glory*. "Let one of us sit at your right hand and the other at your left in your glory" (v. 37).

As I read it, Jesus responds, not with the outrage that feels appropriate to me, but with a kind of gentle resignation. Jesus faces cups of suffering and a baptism of judgment that James and John cannot come close to comprehending, blinded as they are by visions of their own glory.

Predictably, the brothers' rank ambition creates a

rift among the other disciples. The seats of glory are too few for all the disciples to sit in them. Still, the disruption gives Jesus cause to teach on the nobility of leaders who serve and sacrifice. Not only that, Jesus speaks what some have called the central theme of the whole gospel, declaring that he comes "not to be served, but to serve, and to give his life as a ransom for many" (v. 45). This is what Jesus declares to be glorious, the sinless one serving humanity by hanging upon a tree, atoning for the sins of all glory-seekers.

Jesus, forgive us for casting ourselves as heroes in our own "glory stories."

SHOUTING LOUDER
(10:46-52)

*Many rebuked him and told him to be quiet,
but he shouted all the more, "Son of David,
have mercy on me!" (10:48)*

Sometimes, while I'm preaching, I'll notice it out of the corner of my eye. A preschool worker has quietly slipped into the sanctuary, walked to the end of a pew, and gently signaled for a parent to follow her. We all quickly make our assumptions about the backstory. Likely, the workers have tried everything they could think of to calm a crying child—apple juice, crackers, stuffed animals, and pacifiers. But this kid is not having it. He wants one thing and one thing only—his parents.

Now, it's not like the Jericho crowd is trying their best to "comfort" Bartimaeus. This blind man, whose day job was begging along the main road, must have heard snatches of conversation from passersby about Jesus coming through. That's when Bartimaeus cried out the prayer that is at the center of every prayer: "Jesus, son of David, have mercy on me!" (vs. 47). The crowd rebuked him. *Hush up, Jesus has far more important items on his agenda today than the likes of you.* This brings us to one of my favorite phrases in this gospel—"but he shouted all the more..." (vs. 48).

Their attempts to quiet Bartimaeus only stoked the

hunger in his soul. He wanted mercy, and he wanted vision, and ultimately he wanted Jesus (as becomes clear as he immediately follows Jesus after Jesus heals his eyes). The one thing Bartimaeus needed was the one thing only Jesus could provide—"have *mercy* on me."

Jesus, son of David, have mercy on us, too.

One Week That
Towers Above the Others

(MARK 11:1-16:20)

I have never written a biography, but I assume most biographers create these little piles of research on their subjects—ancestors, early life, education, marriage, early career, and so forth. Surely some days are more important than others, and some seasons as well. But the gospel writers are very clear that when it comes to Jesus, one week rules them all. It is the week that gets their most sustained attention. Beginning with what we call Palm Sunday, and moving to that first Easter Sunday, this one week will command a full third of Mark's gospel. As well it should. When I read these words in faith, I begin to understand that, mercifully, my whole life is swallowed up by this week as well.

This is the week Christians call "Holy Week."

PERFECTING
THE CHOREOGRAPHY,
LOSING THE PLOT
(11:1-11)

Those who went ahead and those who followed shouted, "Hosanna!" "Blessed is he who comes in the name of the Lord!" (11:9)

This Palm Sunday passage feels almost like musical theater. The attention to choreography, on the part of Jesus and the disciples and the citizens of Jerusalem, is striking. Jesus asks for the special colt to be brought to him, and this colt becomes the "best supporting actor" (pardon the pun). The disciples take their cloaks, like props, and place them over the donkey. The people too create a "red carpet" of cloaks and branches especially cut for the occasion. They also form a chorus, belting out lines soaked in Biblical significance. Words like "hosanna" and "blessed" and "King David" and "heaven" ring out on the outskirts of Jerusalem. Anyone visiting Jerusalem that day would not fail to miss the pageantry of the occasion. But what is the plot?

Sometimes the Messiah we want is not the Messiah we need. We want David's "son" to defeat this century's Goliath and clean up our town. And while a longing for justice is a noble one, Jesus' journey into Jerusalem that day had an even larger foe in mind. His goal was not to overthrow the political powers of the moment but the collective weight of guilt of all the past, present, and future participants.

"Hosanna!" they shouted, meaning "Save!" The lyric they sang was truer than they knew.

Lord Jesus, you answer our hearts' deepest hosannas.

ALL HAT, NO CATTLE
(11:12-25)

Peter remembered and said to Jesus, "Rabbi, look! The fig tree you cursed has withered!" (11:21)

We tend to remember the sermons we see much longer than the sermons we hear. Jesus gives several visual sermons in our passage. In a typical "sandwich" pattern, Jesus starts and ends with a fig tree. He curses the leafy but fruitless tree one day, and the next morning the disciples discover that the whole tree has withered. In the middle of our text, Jesus essentially curses a fruitless Temple, since its activity is centered more on commerce than on its ancient purpose to be "a house of prayer for all nations" (v. 17). Augustine claimed that the Temple had the leaves (the Law) but not the fruit (mercy).[11]

My country relatives would use a term that was new to this city boy—"a drugstore cowboy." In their estimation, the drugstore cowboy was the rich corporate executive who bought a nearby ranch to play around with on the weekends, complete with the late model pick-up truck and expensive cowboy hat. The only problem was, he wasn't a rancher, and that soon showed. "All hat, no cattle"—as they would say.

I can identify with being a drugstore Christian. I uncomfortably find myself too often in this passage. I can fake the leaves but cannot produce the fruit. I get distracted in God's house and forget the true purpose of why I am there. Like the disciples, I am startled by Christ's judgment (v. 21), but I cling to his promise and his gift of faith, praying that even my great faithlessness might be thrown like a mountain into the heart of the sea (vv. 23-25).

> *Jesus, bring your resurrection power to my*
> *withered heart.*

PLAYING TENNIS
AGAINST JESUS
(11:27-33)

*They discussed it among themselves and said,
"If we say, 'From heaven,' he will ask, 'Then
why didn't you believe him?' But if we say, 'Of
human origin'..." (They feared the people, for
everyone held that John really was a prophet.)
So they answered Jesus, "We don't know." Jesus
said, "Neither will I tell you by what authority
I am doing these things." (11:31–33)*

The back and forth volleys between Jesus and the religious leaders feel like tennis to me. In the previous passage, when Jesus overturned the tables of the moneychangers, Jesus scored an ace. In our passage, the religious powerbrokers come fighting back. They question Jesus about his authority in performing such reckless actions.

Now, the gospel writers are not shy about proclaiming the authority of Jesus. Mark opens this gospel telling us that Jesus is the "Son of God," and at the close of Matthew's gospel Jesus declares, "All authority in heaven and on earth has been given to me" (Matthew 28:18). Still, Jesus returns their serve with a question of his own about the authority inherent in the baptism performed by John the Baptist. This shot sent the religious leaders scrambling. They caucus, trying to manufacture an answer to Jesus' question that will not expose their unbelief on the one hand and fear on the other. Ultimately, they are unable to answer his question. While Jesus wins this game, the religious leaders will soon mount a comeback in the hours leading up to Good Friday.

Meanwhile, the candid discussion of the religious leaders leaves me feeling queasy (vv. 31-"32). How often, behind my pious statements, do unbelief and craven fear challenge the authority of Jesus over me? How desperately do I need Jesus to win the ultimate match?

Jesus, thank you that you ultimately
win the day.

BUILDING ON REJECTION
(12:1-12)

"Haven't you read this passage of Scripture:
'The stone the builders rejected has become the
cornerstone...'" (12:10)

This pointed parable of Jesus is one long series of rejections. A man puts great care into planting a vineyard, and then rents it out. The key word is "rent." Unfortunately, the renters begin to think like owners (and violent ones at that). They assault a servant who has come to collect payment for the vineyard's proceeds. A succession of servants meets a fate of shameful violence or even murder. Finally, the owner sends the last person left—"a son, whom he loved" (v. 6). And in the most treacherous stroke of all, the tenants killed the owner's son, thinking they will have now own the son's inheritance. They didn't even have the decency to bury him within the bounds of his own property. The predictable conclusion of the parable is swift justice for the tenants.

The meaning for those who had seized God's Temple for their own use, for those who followed in the sad history of persecuting God's messengers, could not be more clear. Jesus was serving a warning to his accusers—"the chief priests, the teachers of the law and the elders" (vs. 12). But Jesus was doing more than that. He concludes his dark parable with a line of bright prophecy from Psalm 118: "The stone the builders rejected has become the cornerstone…"

Jesus predicts a "marvelous" reversal of fortunes. The Rejected One, the Owner's Son, the one who was crucified and buried outside the city of Jerusalem, will become the cornerstone of God's renewed people. We are a people built, oddly enough, on rejection.

Jesus, you are our solid foundation.

BENEATH THE CONTROVERSIAL
(12:13-17)

*They brought the coin, and he asked them,
"Whose image is this? And whose inscrip-
tion?" "Caesar's," they replied. Then Jesus said
to them, "Give back to Caesar what is Caesar's and to God what is God's." And they were
amazed at him. (12:16–17)*

No one could say that this was an insignificant question. For centuries, Christians have been trying to figure
out how to cooperate with the state while protecting
their souls. And lots of people love to argue about taxes.
At the same time, Jesus was right to smell a rat. The
two groups that approached him—the morally rigorous
Pharisees and the politically savvy Herodians—were
not exactly ideological brothers. When you add to this
the flattery (v. 14) and the polarizing question (v. 15), it
becomes clear that their gambit was designed to endan-
ger Jesus' standing with either his people or with Rome.

From a debating strategy, Jesus foils their plot by
responding to their either/or question with a both/and
answer: "Give back to Caesar what is Caesar's and to
God what is God's" (v. 17). By his response, Jesus is
likely answering a deeper and unasked question. The
coin is made in the image of Caesar. But what about the
person holding the coin? In whose image is that person

made (Genesis 1:27)?

We are never exempt from hard questions, in life or in church. People with a reputation for erudition and wisdom will still disagree on whether we should cooperate or separate, imbibe or abstain, innovate or conserve. In my experience, however, an excessive engagement in controversy can mask the need to face more personal and painful questions about what God has given to us and what we owe God in return. Such questions cause us to cry out in despair, or cry out for grace.

> *Jesus, forgive us for the many ways we who are made in God's image have failed to give back "to God what is God's."*

WHAT THE SMART DON'T KNOW
(12:18-27)

*"At the resurrection whose wife will she be,
since the seven were married to her?" Jesus
replied, "Are you not in error because you do
not know the Scriptures or the power of God?"
(12:23–24)*

I feel like I've met this Sadducee before. The Sadducees,
by the way, were theological minimalists, known as
much for what they did not believe in—the resurrection, angels, and Jewish writings outside of the Law of
Moses—as what they did. This one is really smart, a bit
mischievous, and his favorite hobby is showing you the
absurdity of your heartfelt beliefs. In this case, he spins
a fanciful tale about an unlucky woman who was married to a succession of seven brothers (after one by one,
the previous brother died). Jesus, if there is such a thing
as a resurrection, as you claim, then you are telling me
when this woman dies she will show up in your mythical
heaven with seven husbands fighting over her?

Jesus responds with one of the most devastating
statements you could ever make to a person who claims
a reputation for theological sophistication. "Your mistake is that you don't know the Scriptures, and you don't
know the power of God" (v. 24, NLT). Jesus then gives
us a window into the life beyond this life, where a God

"of the living" communes with resurrected (and previously married) people.

The Sadducee's question calls to mind for me a nautical tool known as a "ballast"—something weighty required to keep a ship from tipping over. Sometimes, as spiritual vessels, we want to unload what feels like the needless cargo of intellectually challenging doctrines, like the resurrection. If we throw such cargo overboard, we think, we'll be so much lighter and nimble. But could it be that what we are tossing over the edge is an eternal promise of the power of God?

"Christianity begins where religion ends…
with the resurrection." (Herbert
Booth Smith)

WE CAN SEE IT FROM HERE
(12:28-34)

When Jesus saw that he had answered wisely,
he said to him, "You are not far from the king-
dom of God." And from then on no one dared
ask him any more questions. (12:34)

I must admit: at first I had the wrong impression of
this guy. I assumed he was another smiling opponent,
another religious expert using all his rhetorical skills to
trap Jesus. So I was pleasantly surprised when Mark tells
us that this expert was actually drawn to Jesus because
Jesus had given a "good answer" in the previous debate
(v. 28). He asks a frequent question in the gospels. Of
the estimated 613 commandments in the opening books
of Hebrew Scripture, which one towers over the others?

If it were anyone but Jesus answering, we would say
that Jesus cheated by offering two answers instead of
one! He gives us the heart of Israel's faith (Deuteronomy
6:4-5), which urges us to love God with every aspect of
our lives. And then, he pairs it with loving your neigh-
bor with the same intensity we use to love ourselves
(Leviticus 19:18). Jesus gives two commandments, but
both have an otherworldly love at their center.

What follows is a kind of mutual applause. The
expert praises Jesus for highlighting a love that soars
above all the other aspects of our religious activities. Yet

Jesus both applauds and woos the questioner by saying, "You are not far from the kingdom of God" (v. 34). He is so close because he has recognized that the purest form of love is at the heart of our faith. But he will only arrive at the gates of God's kingdom when he realizes that this love, unattainable by flawed humans, will be poured out on us by Christ.

> *Jesus, your love for God and people beckons us*
> *into God's Kingdom.*

JESUS CLIMBS OUT OF OUR BOX
(12:35-37)

David himself, speaking by the Holy Spirit, declared: "The Lord said to my Lord: 'Sit at my right hand until I put your enemies under your feet.'" (12:36)

I've never forgotten an episode of a rather famous 1970s sitcom called "All in the Family." A liberated young woman named Gloria pitches a riddle to her chauvinistic dad (Archie Bunker) about a father and son who are in a car accident. The two victims are rushed to the hospital and wheeled into two separate operating rooms, where two surgeons prep to operate on father and son. But the surgeon who is about to the operate on the boy stops short and says, "I can't operate on him. He's my son!" How can this be? The solution to the riddle—the surgeon was the boy's *mother*—feels painfully obvious on our side of the 21st century. But when I first watched that episode as a child, I was as stumped as Archie. Like him, I had mentally sequestered all surgeons into a box called "Male."

That memory comes rushing back as I read this Q&A from Jesus to the large crowd listening in the Temple Courts. His riddle, on the surface, was not difficult to answer. Why do the teachers of the law refer to the coming Messiah as "the son of David"? "That's easy, Jesus. Multiple prophets foretold that the Messiah would come from the lineage of David." *Yes,* Jesus says, *but do you remember what David himself had to say on the matter in the opening of Psalm 110? David spoke of this future Messiah as "My Lord."*

The reminder is pointed. Our minds want to put Jesus in a clearly marked box. But our "son of David" is also the "son of God," a king who will do for all people what King David could never do. By dying and rising again, Jesus will put all of his enemies (and ours!) under his feet (v. 36).

> *Jesus, forgive us when we shrink you down to categories we can understand.*

THE NECESSITY OF
INTERNAL AFFAIRS
(12:38-40)

*As he taught, Jesus said, "Watch out for the
teachers of the law. They like to walk around
in flowing robes and be greeted with respect in
the marketplaces..." (12:38)*

About 95% of my "expertise" in the area of law enforcement comes from watching cop shows on TV. Still, I'm
pretty certain that most sizable law enforcement agen-
cies have a department called "Internal Affairs." These
men and women essentially *police the police.* They inves-
tigate instances when those who are hired to uphold the
law break the law in the process.

In this passage, Jesus virtually runs a sting operation for "Internal Affairs," only the target is not *civil*
but rather *religious* law enforcers (a.k.a. clergy). As a
card-carrying clergyman, I find these words extremely
painful to hear. Jesus warns against an excessive attention to appearances ("flowing robes"), an obsession with
receiving applause both in church and the community
("greeted with respect in the marketplace"), and a hom-
ing pigeon's vision for locating the seats of power ("the
most important seats in the synagogues and the places
of honor at banquets"). If that's not bad enough, clergy

are often guilty of hiding a pernicious greed under their "lengthy prayers."

This is certainly the sting of the law for people who profess to know God's Word inside and out. And if we broaden the application beyond clergy, I would assume that most readers could identify with a thirst for respect and a hiding of secret sin behind a facade of good Christian piety. When Jesus says that these offenders "will be punished most severely," we throw ourselves at the mercy of our Savior. "Create in me a pure heart, O God" (Psalm 51:10).

Jesus, save us from ourselves.

CHAOS AND THE GOSPEL
(13:1-23)

"You must be on your guard. You will be handed over to the local councils and flogged in the synagogues. On account of me you will stand before governors and kings as witnesses to them. And the gospel must first be preached to all nations. Whenever you are arrested and brought to trial, do not worry beforehand about what to say. Just say whatever is given you at the time, for it is not you speaking, but the Holy Spirit." (13:9–11)

My summary of Jesus' terrifying sermon that opens Mark 13: "If it can be shaken, it will be shaken." World peace will be shaken by wars, and the environment will be (literally) shaken by earthquakes. The church will be shaken by persecution, and families will be shaken by betrayal. Faith will be shaken by desecration and false preaching, and life will be shaken by famine and terror. *Jesus, what gives?*

Jesus' sermon (which many say alternates between a near-term prophecy about the destruction of the Temple and prophecies still to be fulfilled) is prompted by the misplaced confidence of his disciples. Walking among the seemingly immovable "massive stones" of the

Temple (v. 1), Jesus' words strip away every other foundation the disciples might choose to lean upon. Whatever in our life "feels" stable, at the moment, could be undermined by the subversion of evil or the judgment of God. There is one foundation, Jesus preaches, and one alone—Jesus himself is our one cornerstone (see Mark 12:10), his gospel is our one story (13:10), and his Spirit our one strength in chaotic times (13:11).

As I write this, my social media feed has reminded me that six years ago I was doing church under a tree with believers in the beleaguered country of South Sudan. Most had lived as refugees in Uganda for much of their lives. All had seen violence, had lost family members and friends, and some had lost limbs as well. But there they were, under that tree, singing out the gospel.

Jesus, forgive me for leaning on anything else
but you.

TRUSTING WHILE SHAKING
(13:24-31)

*"Heaven and earth will pass away, but my
words will never pass away." (13:31)*

If you are scratching your head after reading this passage, you are not alone—I'm scratching right along with you. These words of Jesus are among the most challenging in the entire gospel of Mark. As with the previous day's reading, Jesus seems to alternate between a futuristic, cosmic judgment (vv. 24-27) and a more near-term act of judgment that "this generation" will experience (v. 30—likely the destruction of the Temple in Jerusalem in A.D. 70). The calamitous indicators of world turmoil that fill this chapter function as signs, like leaves on the fig tree. These scary signs have the ironic impact of reassuring us that the season is about to change and that, ultimately, "people will see the Son of Man coming in clouds with great power and glory" (v. 26).

Regardless of your interpretation of the many apocalyptic references in this chapter, I hope you will agree that Jesus is teaching his followers a counterintuitive response to chaos. When life falls apart (and when our world falls apart), we naturally feel ourselves falling with it. After all, the guardrails on the Titanic are useless when the Titanic itself is sinking.

Yet Jesus states that chaos is actually a harbinger of

rescue, as surely as Good Friday is followed by Easter Sunday. Let go of the guardrails of this sinking world, and grab hold of the gospel words of Jesus. "Heaven and earth will pass away, but my words will never pass away."

Jesus, steady us with your gospel promises.

WHAT TIME IS IT?
(13:32-37)

"It's like a man going away: He leaves his house and puts his servants in charge, each with their assigned task, and tells the one at the door to keep watch. Therefore keep watch because you do not know when the owner of the house will come back—whether in the evening, or at midnight, or when the rooster crows, or at dawn." (13:34–35)

In the parable that closes the dark and challenging sermon in Chapter 13, Jesus gives us two ways to think about time. In one scenario, the Master owns it all, including time itself. And so, even if the Master is long gone and it feels like he's never coming back, I still retain my identity as his servant and my duty to perform my "assigned task" in a daily fashion (v. 34). In other words, I am always on the clock.

A second way to think about time is that the Master has basically abandoned us, and for all practical purposes may be dead or have given up on us. And so, I begin to think less like a servant and more like an owner. I begin to act with lethargy rather with urgency. I look at my house, my job, my family, and my life with a sense of entitlement—these people and belongings are here to serve me. I have all the time in the world to spend in the manner of my choosing.

At the church where I work, I have inhabited my lovely office for about 15 years. Sometimes, when I am searching for something in the back of a drawer, I'll come across an old "Palm Pilot" or CD-ROM of a long-abandoned software program. In truth, I have sat in that desk for so long I sometimes absentmindedly assume it is *my* desk. It is not. I don't own it any more than I own my job title. It is a gift, loaned out to me, technically by my church but ultimately by my Master. And my time given to sit and serve from that desk is truly a gift of grace.

Lord, forgive me for stealing time
away from you.

THE GOSPEL, ILLUSTRATED
AND APPRAISED
(14:1-11)

"Leave her alone," said Jesus. "Why are you bothering her? She has done a beautiful thing to me." (14:6)

What stands out to me most in this strange and wonderful passage is Jesus' ability to focus on the essential in the midst of dark distractions. The heart of the story is slipped between conspiratorial meetings, with Judas Iscariot ultimately signing up to be the linchpin of a plot to seize Jesus (vv. 1-2, 10-11). An unnamed woman initiates an action that feels at the very least to be horribly inappropriate behavior for a dinner party. She takes "an alabaster jar of very expensive perfume" (v. 3) (likely the equivalent of her retirement fund) and pours the contents of the broken jar on the head of Jesus. Her strange behavior incites indignant lectures from the guests about waste and social responsibility.

Jesus, in the chaos of conspiracy and awkwardness and indignation, focuses the attention of his dinner companions (and us!) on the sheer beauty of the woman's service. He reads into her action a gift that may have exceeded the woman's loving intentions—a preparation for his upcoming burial. And then, in an act of stunning humility, Jesus writes this woman's story as an appendix to the central gospel story: "Truly I tell you, wherever the gospel is preached throughout the world, what she has done will also be told, in memory of her" (v. 9).

The story of Jesus *is* the story of the gospel. Jesus need not share the limelight with anyone else. But how like Jesus to notice and appraise gospel-ish acts of courage, humility, and costly love, and to package them with the ultimate story of humble and courageous love poured out for all.

Jesus, your broken body is our alabaster jar.

ME?
(14:12-21)

*When evening came, Jesus arrived with the
Twelve. While they were reclining at the table
eating, he said, "Truly I tell you, one of you will
betray me—one who is eating with me." They
were saddened, and one by one they said to
him, "Surely you don't mean me?" (14:17–19)*

On the heels of the conspiracy to capture him, Jesus
moves into stealth mode—enlisting two disciples to
help secure a safe place for one last gathering with his
disciples. Jesus instructs them to locate a mysterious
man carrying a water jar (a job usually done by women)
to lead them to the ample upper room for the obser-
vance of Passover. It is there, around the Passover table,
with its various courses and carbs and proteins with
their sauces, that Jesus drops his bombshell—"one of
you will betray me—one who is eating with me" (v. 18).
The disciples were filled with grief, to be sure, but not
only grief. We are also told that "one by one" they asked,
"Surely you don't mean me?"

I have had the excruciating experience of sitting
on a jury for a criminal trial. I listened to evidence
and counter-evidence about the defendant's guilt, and
passed his family members in the hall outside the court-
room. We jurors were commissioned to sift through the

evidence and make a judgment about another person's guilt (and indeed, their destiny). Yet the prediction Jesus makes takes my angst to a whole new level. The disciples have to play jurors analyzing the potential of their own hearts. *Is it I? Am I capable of doing something so horrible?*

Technically, for eleven of the disciples at least, the answer is "no." Judas Iscariot will bear responsibility for that sad fate. Yet if we look at the question more broadly, if we think about all the different ways someone can betray Jesus, the answer is a sad and silent "yes."

Jesus, reveal to me the sin of betrayal that
currently hides itself from me.

THE HIDDEN MENU
(14:22-26)

While they were eating, Jesus took bread, and when he had given thanks, he broke it and gave it to his disciples, saying, "Take it; this is my body." (14:22)

Of the hundreds of meals Jesus had shared with his disciples over a three-year period, this is the one that would stand out the most. Jesus took a meal that was already significant—the commemoration of judgment "passing over" Israel as they prepared for their Exodus from captivity in Egypt—and took it to a completely new level. I wonder how the disciples reacted when Jesus altered the traditional script of the Jewish Passover? After all, he called the bread "my body," and the cup "my blood of the covenant, which is poured out for many." The disciples no doubt *thought* they had ordered off the normal, Passover menu. The unleavened bread and wine appeared to be the same as their ancestors had consumed on this night down through the centuries. But now, Jesus is revealing a new and hidden menu.

One of the slurs against the early church by her opponents was that they were cannibals. Reading this passage, you can see how that rumor got started. *Those Christians say they eat his body and drink his blood!* And Christians have certainly argued and theologized through the centuries about exactly *how* Christ is consumed, complete with dueling six-syllable words.

Still, one cannot escape the sheer grace of this incident. Jesus the Host is also Jesus the Main Course. The meal he offers will be consumed by undeserving friends around his table.

Jesus, you are the main course our souls crave.

THE FAILURE OF BEST
INTENTIONS
(14:27-31)

Peter declared, "Even if all fall away, I will not." "Truly I tell you," Jesus answered, "to-day—yes, tonight—before the rooster crows twice you yourself will disown me three times." (14:29–30)

If you have read the gospels before, you may have this sense of foreboding as the disciples walk with Jesus from the Upper Room to the Garden of Gethsemane. Darkness is quickly falling and hope fading. Jesus reinforces the gloom when he shares the ancient prophecy from Zechariah about a struck shepherd and scattered sheep, predicting the disaster about to befall him and his disciples. Still, Jesus manages to hold out this flickering promise that he will rise and be united with his friends (v. 28).

Peter, predictably, will not hear of it! "Even if all fall away, I will not" (v. 29). Sadly, Jesus predicts that Peter's resolve will have quickly melted away before the night is over. To describe Peter's defection, Jesus uses that horrible word "disown," which Peter will do not once but three times. What emotions fill Jesus' heart at this moment? Surely deep disappointment and despair, but what else?

My son Jack is in grad school, pursuing a career in higher education. When he was in preschool, he used to promise me that he was going to become a pilot and live next door to me when he grew up. And every day he was going to walk over to my house and say, "Where do you want to fly to today, Dad?" That memory helps me marvel at the wise and tender love in the heart of Jesus, which in that moment can forgive Peter for the failure of his best intentions.

Jesus, forgive us for our massive failure to live up to our ambitious promises.

TEARS ABOUNDING
(14:32-42)

Going a little farther, he fell to the ground and prayed that if possible the hour might pass from him. "Abba, Father," he said, "everything is possible for you. Take this cup from me. Yet not what I will, but what you will." (14:35–36)

The first time I stepped into the Garden of Gethsemane, I saw a group of women kneeling around an ancient olive tree, praying and weeping. I wasn't prepared for that. As I reflect upon the combined impressions of that memory and my reading of this passage, it is difficult to narrow down the causes for weeping.

Did they weep tears of remorse over human *frailty*? Jesus could not have been clearer—especially with his inner circle of Peter, James, and John—that this was the most important prayer meeting of their lives. Jesus needed their prayerful companionship, and their own souls needed the fortification of prayer as well. But unfortunately, "their eyes were heavy" (v. 40).

Did they weep tears of sorrow over human *willfulness*? How many times have I essentially prayed what you might call the reverse-Gethsemane prayer? "Father, your will is pretty clear in this area. Nevertheless, not what *you* will, but what *I* will. *My* will be done."

Did they weep tears of shame over human *guilt*?

Did they get some glimpse into the enormity of Jesus' mission? All of our collective shame bearing down upon Jesus' head in that moment?

Or were these tears of joy? In that garden, surrounded by olive trees like the ones where I watched women kneel, Jesus resolved to do what had to be done to redeem us. Tears are the order of the day.

Jesus, my destiny turns on your decision in Gethsemane.

LIKE REBELS QUASHING
A REBELLION
(14:43-52)

"Am I leading a rebellion," said Jesus, "that you have come out with swords and clubs to capture me?" (14:48)

This sad reading could be an advertisement for the doctrine of "total depravity." No mere human comes away looking good in this passage. The religious royalty (chief priests, esteemed teachers, wise elders) have sent an armed mob to arrest Jesus. One of those Jesus has poured his life into for three years, Judas, betrays Jesus with a fake greeting and a sinister kiss. One of Jesus' disciples (whom John identifies as Peter), likely aims a sword for a guard's neck and manages to slice off his ear. And what of the rest of those who were not complicit in Jesus' betrayal or arrest? "Then everyone deserted him and fled" (v. 50). The last one fleeing is an unnamed "young man," whose linen garment is seized and who manages to escape with his life and little else (vv. 51-52). Many believe this young man is actually Mark, our author.

Jesus asks, "Am I leading a rebellion?" (v. 48) Quite the opposite. Jesus is betrayed by rebels, those who play for different teams but end up uniting to fight against him. Jesus is betrayed by those who fight against God's holy law, those who give into "fight or flight" (or, in Peter's case, both).

There can be only one bright spot in this literally and spiritually dark time. Jesus is fulfilling the Hebrew Scriptures. Jesus is fulfilling his ancient calling. As Isaiah 53:8 put it, "*By oppression and judgment he was taken away. Yet who of his generation protested? For he was cut off from the land of the living; for the transgression of my people he was punished.*"

Jesus, you came to rebel against our rebellion.

A VERDICT IN SEARCH OF
A RATIONALE
(14:53-65)

*But Jesus remained silent and gave no answer.
Again the high priest asked him, "Are you the
Messiah, the Son of the Blessed One?" "I am,"
said Jesus. "And you will see the Son of Man
sitting at the right hand of the Mighty One
and coming on the clouds of heaven." The high
priest tore his clothes. "Why do we need any
more witnesses?" he asked. (14:61–63)*

Here's the sentence that grabs me. "The chief priests and
the whole Sanhedrin were looking for evidence against
Jesus so that they could put him to death, *but they did
not find any*" (v. 55). At first, the chief religious officers in
Israel look ridiculous. One of the advantages of giving
false statements is that in theory you can make them
harmonize, but not so in Jesus' trial (v. 56). Another wit-
ness twisted a statement Jesus had once made about his
own body as the true temple (John 2:19-22), making it
seem as if Jesus hatched a plot to destroy the *literal* temple. When the high priest tried to get Jesus to interact
with the lies aimed in his direction, he chose instead to
remain silent.

When a straight question was put to Jesus, however,
he found the timing right to reveal his true identity. All

throughout this gospel, Jesus has been waiting for that perfect, awful time to pull back the curtain on himself. "Are you the Messiah?" the High Priest asks. Jesus not only says yes, but prophesies that they will see him in his regal glory. What all the false witnesses could not do, Jesus did himself. He gave them the reason they were looking for to condemn him as "worthy of death" (v. 64). Beatings and humiliations soon followed (v. 65)

This is sheer chaos. The keepers of Israel's religion recklessly break commandments and blaspheme, while the Sinless One stands condemned.

Jesus, you were broken by the hands of
religious people like me.

THE TRAGEDY OF
REGRESSION
(14:66-72)

Immediately the rooster crowed the second time. Then Peter remembered the word Jesus had spoken to him: "Before the rooster crows twice you will disown me three times." And he broke down and wept. (14:72)

In the app store on my smart phone, I can download a number of apps that promise to take me from the "couch" of inactivity to running a 5K in a number of weeks. The reviews of the better-known apps feature testimonials of people (likely with younger knees than mine) who did precisely that. They made the decision to work out, began by running merely to the edge of their driveway, and ended up running a full five kilometers. Bully for them!

We would love for our life with Jesus to work the same way. In our earliest days with Jesus, we were spiritual weaklings. *But look at us now—what impressive spiritual specimens we have become*! Peter's story paints a darker picture. This man who has "worked out" with Jesus every day (for three years!), who has just promised to die with him (v. 31), is now isolated and afraid. He lurks in the courtyard just outside the farcical religious trial Jesus is presently enduring. And when Peter is presented with an opportunity to profess his undying love and death-embracing allegiance to Jesus, he denies his Lord with the strongest language possible. Three times. Ultimately, Peter says of his Lord: "I don't know this man you're talking about." When the rooster crows, Peter remembers Jesus' terrible prophecy.

When Christians preach the "good news," it is not the news of our unfailing progress to make good on the grace Christ has given us. After all, Peter denied he even *knew* Jesus. But on the cross, Jesus does not deny that he knows us.

> *"O Lord Jesus Christ, look upon us with those eyes of thine where-with thou didst look upon Peter in the hall; that with Peter we may repent and, by the same love be forgiven; for thy mercy's sake. Amen." (Lancelot Andrews)*

THE SWAP
(15:1-15)

"Do you want me to release to you the king of the Jews?" asked Pilate, knowing it was out of self-interest that the chief priests had handed Jesus over to him. But the chief priests stirred up the crowd to have Pilate release Barabbas instead. (15:9–11)

How is it that a holy man is condemned while a murderer is set free? This could only happen through a grand collusion of evil. First, we have the conspiracy of the religious leaders, who "made their plans" to utilize the hated Roman government as an instrument to get rid of Jesus. Second, these same religious leaders managed to exploit the fickleness of the crowd and "stirred" them up in irrational hatred of Jesus. Finally, the political cowardice of the Roman governor Pilate caused him to go against his own conscience (v. 14) and "satisfy the crowd" by handing Jesus over for crucifixion (v. 15). There it is—conspiracy, rage, and expediency colluded to condemn Jesus to death.

And what about the murderer? Justice rightly has him sitting in jail, awaiting capital punishment for crimes of insurrection and murder. The Law of Moses was pretty clear on the subject: "Whoever sheds human blood, by humans shall their blood be shed; for in the

image of God has God made mankind." (Genesis 9:6).
The murderer Barabbas likely hears the footsteps of
the Law coming toward him that fateful Good Friday
morning, waiting to administer justice and take him to
his crucifixion. Blood for blood—that's what the law
decrees.

But on this particular day, those jangling keys sing
a song of freedom. And not just for Barabbas. My sins
imprison me in my own cell of condemnation. But here
comes Jesus, twirling those keys.

> *"That is the mystery which is rich in divine*
> *grace to sinners: wherein by a wonderful ex-*
> *change our sins are no longer ours but Christ's*
> *and the righteousness of Christ not Christ's*
> *but ours." (Martin Luther)*

A RIDICULOUS PLACE FOR A WORSHIP SERVICE
(15:16-21)

They put a purple robe on him, then twisted together a crown of thorns and set it on him. And they began to call out to him, "Hail, king of the Jews!" (15:17–18)

This may sound far-fetched, but go with me. If you knew nothing about the gospels, and you saw this scene from *very* far off, you might mistake it for a worship service. People are gathered together in an important place, where a central figure is draped in royal purple and receives what appears to be a crown upon his head. And though you can't quite make out the words, the people seem to be acclaiming him with shouts of admiration at the very least, if not outright praise. And while your total view of the event is obscured, you can definitely make out people kneeling and bowing low before this central figure.

Move closer, and what briefly felt like worship now turns your stomach. The mockery of false praise can sting more than the blunt force of outright contempt. The robe is temporary, the crown has thorny spikes embedded in it, and the pseudo-praise is laced with true scorn and violence (before Jesus is ultimately led out for crucifixion). This is anti-worship, poisoned worship, demonic worship.

Yet move closer still. Regardless of the mocking intent, a true king stands before us, and no mocking words can change that fact. See the love etched in pain upon his face. This king is on a valiant mission to save us, even from ourselves.

"Did e'er such love and sorrow meet, or thorns compose so rich a crown?" (Isaac Watts)

FOR ALL THE WORLD TO SEE
(15:21-32)

It was nine in the morning when they crucified him. The written notice of the charge against him read: THE KING OF THE JEWS. *(15:25–26)*

The Romans designed the uniquely cruel punishment of crucifixion as deterrence. Accordingly, it was not performed in some out-of-view bunker for a private audience of law enforcement professionals. Instead, its victims were elevated high into the air, like actors on an open-air stage, spreading its "crime does not pay" message to the broadest circumference of citizens.

And so, this most horrible and most central event of holy history takes place for all to see. What do we observe? Surely we cannot miss *humanity at its worst.* Jesus' hands and feet are run through with spikes. A wholly innocent Jesus is visually lumped together with notorious criminals who hang on either side of him. Soldiers roll dice to see who gets the clothes that have been stripped from him. A sign ("THE KING OF THE JEWS") is affixed over his head, and passersby take turns "hurling" their worst insults at him. The common theme of the insults is that if Jesus was truly who he claimed to be, he would not be hanging powerless from the cross.

My prayer is that we who have read this gospel from the beginning see something else—*Jesus' love for humanity at her worst.* The chief priests claimed—"he saved others, but he cannot save himself" (v. 31). More truly, out of love, Jesus saves others by choosing *not* to save himself. The Romans preached that crime does not pay, but Christ preaches that he will pay for every cosmic offense we have ever committed. This is the gospel in its most pure and public essence.

Jesus, you saved us by refusing to save yourself.

EVERYBODY'S TALKING
(15:33-39)

Someone ran, filled a sponge with wine vine-
gar, put it on a staff, and offered it to Jesus to
drink. "Now leave him alone. Let's see if Eli-
jah comes to take him down," he said. (15:36)

As Jesus dies, everybody's talking. Jesus, in his anguish,
prays a line from Psalm 22 ("My God, my God, why
have you forsaken me?"), and later utters a "loud cry"
with his final breath. Bystanders misunderstand the
Aramaic phrase *Eloi* ("my God") for the Old Testament
prophet Elijah. If you've ever sung or heard "Swing Low,
Sweet Chariot," you were singing about Elijah's majestic
exit from this earth. So some wondered aloud: *Is that*
what Jesus is expecting? Elijah to bring his chariot and res-
cue him from this horror? And others scoffed: *Ha! Let's*
just see if Elijah shows up! Curiously, a Roman centurion
speaks. By all rights, the last person we would imagine
having a profound theological insight on this day gives
one of the clearest interpretations of this event—this
persecuted criminal is in fact God's son.

In his own way, Jesus' Father is speaking. The miraculous darkness that covers the land paints an appropriate backdrop for the cosmic sorrow that accompanies Jesus' crucifixion. The Father also speaks through
a visual and audible parable, the tearing of the curtain

that (formerly) separated the holy presence of God from sinful women and men.

Everybody's talking, and our job is to listen. We listen to the God-forsakenness of the Son of God, who refuses Elijah's rescue and dies as the condemned substitute for our aggregate sin and shame. And we listen for the tearing of the curtain, knowing that through the cross our welcome into God's holy presence is now complete.

Jesus, you were forsaken that we might be forgiven.

PREPARATION DAY
(15:43-47)

*Joseph of Arimathea, a prominent member of
the Council, who was himself waiting for the
kingdom of God, went boldly to Pilate and
asked for Jesus' body. (15:43)*

If true love asks for nothing in return, then in this passage true love is on display. Prominent followers of Jesus (many of whom have a "Mary" in their name) have kept vigil with Jesus "from a distance" as he hangs upon the cross. These and a host of other women are emotionally and spiritually present with Jesus during his final moments. Two of the Marys even follow Jesus' body to the tomb so that they might mark the spot and later return to honor his body.

Curiously, not only do the Marys play a role in Jesus' burial but so does a Joseph. Joseph of Arimathea (a member of the Sanhedrin, which condemned Jesus) summons the courage to petition Pilate for Jesus' body. He releases Jesus' naked body from the cross, adorns it in linen, and secures it behind a stone in what was likely a new tomb cut for Joseph's own family. Such was the impact of Christ's gracious love for every Mary and Joseph.

Mark calls the Friday on which Jesus died "Preparation Day" (v. 42)—preparation for the Sabbath rest on the following day. Yet could any of Jesus' closest followers have known that the day of his death was a *preparation day* for his resurrection? That the only thing "final" about this day is that their sins were finally and completely forgiven? How do you *prepare* for a life-altering day like that? As I reflect on this passage, I find myself deeply cheered by the fact that even my worst day can be a *preparation day* for the work of the risen Christ in the midst of brokenness and grief.

Jesus, who knows what you are graciously
preparing for us on this day?

THE BEAUTY OF
A FAILED ERRAND
(16:1-8)

*"But go, tell his disciples and Peter, 'He is going
ahead of you into Galilee. There you will see
him, just as he told you.'" Trembling and bewildered, the women went out and fled from
the tomb. They said nothing to anyone, because
they were afraid. (16:7–8)*

Afterwards, the three women who made the very-ear-
ly-morning walk to the tomb must have reflected on
the fact that nothing was successful about their original
errand. They brought spices with them, not to embalm
the body, but to function like an air freshener, to dis-
tract their noses from the unmistakable stench of death.
These spices were never used. As they walked in the
dark, the biggest fear on their minds was whom they
could find to help roll away the impossibly large stone
that guarded the entrance to Jesus' tomb. That problem
was never faced. The goal of their mission was to find a
corpse, but a corpse was never found.

Instead, the women found an open tomb, a missing body, and a "young man" who certainly must have
been an angel...and a gospel preacher. In a brief and
brilliant sermon, the angel hits so many key parts of the
gospel message—the crucifixion, the resurrection, the

commission to share the good news, and the promise of a reunion with Jesus. Oh, and one more thing: "do not be alarmed." Some sermons take a while to sink in, I guess, because everything about the final verse of Mark's original gospel smells of fear. "*Trembling and bewildered, the women went out and fled from the tomb. They said nothing to anyone, because they were afraid*" (v. 8).

Later, as we know from the other gospels, these women found their courage and their voice. Still, it is hard to imagine a more honest initial response to the good news of Easter. We come to church on Easter Sunday, preparing to pay our respects to our memory of a moribund faith, but end up running out of church ashen-faced, silent, hearts racing at the immensity of the newly-understood news.

Jesus, may you always bring our dying hope
back to life.

FREEZE FRAME
(16:9-20)

He said to them, "Go into all the world and
preach the gospel to all creation." (16:15)

In my Bible, the words in Mark 16:9-20 are set off by
a near-page-length dividing line and rendered in ital-
ics, in order to signify that "the earliest manuscripts and
some other ancient witnesses" did not include these
words in Mark's original gospel. Because the bulk of
what is described there is captured well in other gospels,
I'll choose to let the final verse in the previous reading
be the final words for our consideration: "*Trembling and
bewildered, the women went out and fled from the tomb.
They said nothing to anyone, because they were afraid*" (v.
8).

Sometimes, when my wife and I are watching a
Netflix drama together, one of us will ask the other to
pause it. Maybe one of us needs a restroom break or
wants to grab a snack. Maybe one of us wants the other
to answer a question about what has gone before in the
show, to make sure we are fully prepared for the scene
that is about to take place.

The ending of Mark's original gospel seems like a
freeze-frame. The image of women fleeing frightened
from the tomb is frozen in time. Perhaps such is the
case for everyone who truly confronts the horror of the

crucifixion and the stunning news of the resurrection. For a moment, everything stops.

But then, afterwards, our life is un-paused as faith pushes us forward, and Jesus is waiting, "just as he told you" (v. 7).

> *Jesus, un-pause our faith that we might experience your resurrected presence.*

Afterword

If you have made it to the very end, I want to congratulate you! Mark began his gospel by speaking about the "beginning" of the good news of Jesus, and you have had a chance to see for yourself (perhaps for the first time) that the news about Jesus is truly good. He is good, and his message is good, and his loving death on your behalf and God's resurrection of him from the dead comprise the best news of all. I pray these stories and words of Jesus will linger with you, even the hard ones. I pray you will rehearse them and muse on them and puzzle over them and celebrate them. And I pray that for you, too, this good news is only the beginning.

ENDNOTES

1. Unless otherwise noted, all Scripture in this book is NIV.

2. *Preachers on Preaching*, from *The Christian Century*, "Episode 27: Paul Scott Wilson," May 8, 2016.

3. *The Guardian*, "William Trevor, watchful master of the short story, dies aged 88," November 21, 2016.

4. from the hymn, "Jesus, Thou Joy of Loving Hearts"

5. Eugene H. Peterson, *The Jesus Way*. (Grand Rapids: Eerdmans, 2007), 8.

6. Ann Patchett, *The Getaway Car*.

7. Chrysostom: "And even apart from reading the Gospel, in assemblies and meetings at home or in the market, in every place…even to the very ends of the earth, you will hear this voice and see that righteous man even now still crying out, resounding loudly, reproving the evil of the tyrant. He will never be silenced nor the reproof at all weakened by the passing of time."

8. Big Think, "The Science of Close-Talkers Revealed," by Andrew Moseman.

9. Flagging this use of the English Standard Version, if permissions are necessary.

10. Flannery O'Connor, *Mystery and Manners: Occasional Prose*, 34.

11. *Mark (Ancient Christian Commentary on Scripture)* by Thomas C. Oden, Christopher A. Hall.

ACKNOWLEDGEMENTS

For years I have frequently described myself to friends as a "wannabe writer." In using that designation, I think I was not just letting others know that I was an English major in college and have a deep affection for words beautifully rendered. I think I was trying to somehow intimate that there was an uncertain "author" hidden deep within my psyche, like a frightened kitten that accidentally slipped into your garage and refuses to come out from under the workbench.

For that reason, I am profoundly grateful for all those, too many to name, who have conspired to coax me out into the wide world of writing. I would like to single out the support of Valley Ranch Baptist Church, and all of her members and leaders who actively encouraged me to write and created space in my schedule to do so. I want to thank specifically my friend Jeff Lamb, who once lovingly told me that I was wasting my time trying to craft literary emails and needed to channel that energy in a more helpful direction. I am indebted to fellow pastor and friend Dr. Andy McQuitty for serving as a writing partner on a once-and-future book project. Dean Todd Still of Truett Seminary and Dr. Scot McKnight from Northern Seminary also contributed timely words of support and advice.

I will also never forget the day when providence assigned me a seat next to Rev. Aaron Zimmerman at a now defunct committee the two of us served on through Baylor University. Aaron introduced me to Mockingbird Ministries (where he currently serves as president of the board). I became an instant fan of all things Mockingbird—blogposts, magazines, podcasts, video, audio, and conferences. I count the day that Mockingbird added me to their list of contributors as an especially bright one, and the day they emailed me a book contract an even more glorious one. To David Zahl, Ethan Richardson, and especially to my editor C.J. Green, your wise counsel and continuous affirmation have been a source of deep joy.

Lastly I wish to honor my wife Jaletta. She was my first editor, a fellow lover of fine writing, a deep well of wisdom, and Exhibit A of those the apostle Peter calls "faithful stewards of God's grace in its various forms" (1 Peter 4:10).

ABOUT THE AUTHOR

Larry Parsley is the senior pastor of Valley Ranch Baptist Church in Dallas, Texas. He is a native of Corpus Christi, and holds degrees from Baylor University (BA, Ph.D.) and Southwestern Seminary (M.Div.). He and his wife Jaletta are the proud parents of Drew, Jack, Timothy, and Laurel.

ABOUT MOCKINGBIRD

Founded in 2007, Mockingbird is an organization devoted to connecting the Christian faith with the realities of everyday life in fresh and down-to-earth ways. We do this primarily, but not exclusively, through our publications, conferences, and online resources. To find out more, visit us at mbird.com or e-mail us at info@ mbird.com.

ALSO FROM MOCKINGBIRD

The Mockingbird Quarterly

Unmapped:
A Spiritual Memoir Duet
by Charlotte Getz & Stephanie Phillips

Law and Gospel: A Theology for
Sinners (and Saints)
by Will McDavid, Ethan Richardson, and David Zahl

A Mess of Help
From the Crucified Soul of Rock
N'Roll
by David Zahl

Eden and Afterward: A
Mockingbird Guide to Genesis
by Will McDavid

Grace in Addiction:
The Good News of Alcoholics
Anonymous for Everybody
by John Z.

The Mockingbird Devotional:
Good News for Today (and
Everyday)

More Theology & Less Heavy
Cream

The Man Who Met God in a Bar:
A Novel

Bed & Board: Plain Talk About
Marriage

Exit 36: A Fictional Chronicle
by Robert Farrar Capon

The Very Persistent Pirate
by CJ & Maddy Green

Churchy: The Real Life Adventures
of a Wife, Mom, and Priest
by Sarah Condon

Mockingbird at the Movies

PZ's Panopticon:
An Off-the-Wall Guide to World
Religion

Our books are available at mbird.com/publications or on
Amazon, and our quarterly magazine can be found at maga-
zine.mbird.com.